India before Alexander

Also by the author:
Vedic Physics: Scientific Origin of Hinduism
India after Alexander: The Age of Vikramādityas
India after Vikramāditya: The Melting Pot

India before Alexander
A New Chronology

Raja Ram Mohan Roy, Ph.D.

Mount Meru Publishing

Published in 2015 by:
Mount Meru publishing
P.O. Box 30026
Cityside Postal Outlet PO
Mississauga, Ontario
Canada L4Z 0B6
Email: mountmerupublishing@gmail.com

ISBN 978-0-9684120-4-6

Dedicated to Swāmī Vivekānanda (1863-1902),
whose words of wisdom have inspired me all my life.

CONTENTS

PREFACE

I have deep respect for and a profound curiosity about ancient Indian civilization. I don't think of myself as an individual who was given birth some 50 years ago. I think of myself as a continuation of a thought process and a civilizational effort that began some 5000 years ago in the valleys of the Saraswatī River. I came to this world in the arms of a living tradition, which continues to nourish me with the wisdom accumulated over five millennia. I have always felt that I have a duty to understand, explore, and comment on this civilizational effort.

Civilizations have flowered and floundered, and when we use the expression "flower", we have to understand that like delicate flowers, civilizations too need nourishment and protection. Just because a civilization has survived the vicissitudes of time does not guarantee that it is going to continue to survive. Ancient Indian civilization has survived because our ancestors empowered it with the insights and knowledge gained through penance and perseverance. Today, the legacy of my ancestors is under great strain – from forces within and without.

I grew up having the deepest respect for my ancestors only to be taught in school later that they were invaders who had destroyed the native Indian civilization and enslaved the native people. I have doubted the veracity of these claims and wondered if it was a lie manufactured to "divide and rule" India. It has been my earnest desire to critically examine the evidence to figure out the truth.

It was in 2001 that I started reading and writing about India's past. As I researched, it became clear to me how the invasion of India by Alexander the Great has been used as a sheet anchor to fix the chronology of Indian history. I also realized that this invasion was close to the midpoint of the 5,000 year old Indian civilization. It then occurred to me to name my books "India before Alexander: A New Chronology" and "India after Alexander: The Age of Vikramādityas".

My wife Manju has given me the love and support to sustain this long-time passion and effort. I would like to thank Dr. Surjeet and Romila Sira for their encouragement and financial support towards publishing this book. I would also like to express my sincere gratitude to Prof. Ramesh Rao for editorial comments and suggestions.

Raja Ram Mohan Roy
Mississauga, Ontario, Canada
August 2015

TRANSLITERATION GUIDE

अ	a	आ	ā		
इ	i	ई	ī		
उ	u	ऊ	ū	ऋ	ṛ
ए	e	ऐ	ai		
ओ	o	औ	au		
अं	ṃ	अः	ḥ		
क	k	ख	kh		
ग	g	घ	gh	ङ	ṅ
च	ch*	छ	chh*		
ज	j	झ	jh	ञ	ñ
ट	ṭ	ठ	ṭh		
ड	ḍ	ढ	ḍh	ण	ṇ
त	t	थ	th		
द	d	ध	dh	न	n
प	p	फ	ph		
ब	b	भ	bh	म	m
य	y	र	r		
ल	l	व	v		
श	ś	ष	ṣ	स	s
ह	h	क्ष	kṣ	त्र	tr
ज्ञ	jñ	श्र	śr		

*Slightly different from International Alphabet of Sanskrit Transliteration scheme.

"Time goes by so fast, people go in and out of your life. You must never miss the opportunity to tell these people how much they mean to you."

- Alexander Graham Bell

1. ONCE UPON A TIME

"Study Sanskrit, but along with it study western sciences as well. Learn accuracy, my boys, study and labour so that the time will come when you can put our history on a scientific basis. For now Indian history is disorganised. The histories of our country written by English writers cannot but be weakening to our minds, for, they talk only of our downfall. How can foreigners, who understand very little of our manners and customs, or of our religion and philosophy, write faithful and unbiased histories of India? Naturally many false notions and wrong inferences have found their way into them. Nevertheless they have shown us how to proceed making researches into our ancient history. Now it is for us to strike out an independent path of historical research for ourselves, to study the Vedas and Puranas and the ancient annals (Itihāsas) of India, and from them make it your life's sādhanā (disciplined endeavour) to write accurate, sympathetic and soul-inspiring histories of the land. It is for Indians to write Indian History. Therefore, set yourselves to the task of rescuing our lost and hidden treasures from oblivion. Even as one's child has been lost does not rest until one has found it, so do you never cease to labour until you have revived the glorious past of India in the consciousness of the people. That will be the true national education, and with its advancement, a true national spirit will be awakened." [1]

These words, and this call for action by Swāmī Vivekānanda explain the motivation for writing this book, and I invite you on this journey into India's remote past seeking his blessings. I urge you to keep an open mind since history has been the narration of partial and partisan telling, and nothing can be considered as established till carefully verified, and even after verification subject to change based on new evidence. Every event and idea is and should be open to scrutiny. The history of India is constructed through variety and a patchwork of sources, and the linear tale sought to be woven by modern historians is the result of the ideologies and the training regimen that emerged from forces and movements seeking to establish their supremacy over people they conquered and sought to subdue. Agenda driven as it is, the information contained in the "histories" of India can be true, partially true or false. There is no need to believe any source, as each one of them is constrained by both their motivation and their limitations. Given that India is an ancient land, occupied by and fought over for millennia we can expect Hindu sources to have their own agenda, while Buddhists, Muslims, Christians, European colonialists, and modern ideologues like the Left-Marxist historians have their own. It is therefore important to consider and examine each piece of information critically to arrive at conclusions that have the highest degree of probability to have actually happened. A narrative that connects carefully the action, the actors, and the plots in the myriad and seminal events can then offer the reader a coherent history of India, open for verification surely but also authentic.

History deals with events, ideas and people, and they need to be recorded, interpreted, and authenticated. Depending on who is doing these, the history of any people can be easily perverted. The distortion of history could be a result of either interpretation and logical fallacies or factual mistakes and inaccuracies. In this volume and subsequent books in the series ("India after Alexander:

The Age of Vikramādityas" and "India after Vikramāditya: The Melting Pot"), I am not going to focus much attention on the biased interpretation of Indian history. My efforts are directed towards unravelling major factual inaccuracies. In other words, instead of discussing what a stated event really meant, I will be discussing whether the stated event actually took place. To do this, it is imperative that events be separated from interpretations and analyzed afresh objectively by consulting original sources.

1.1 The Way we were

Let us start with a paper titled "On the Chronology of the Hindus", by Sir William Jones (1788 CE) [2]. Jones made phenomenal contributions to the field of Indology. He was the founding member of the Asiatick Society, later called Asiatic Society of Bengal. The Asiatick Society published the journal "*Asiatick Researches*" as part of its mandate. Jones noted the similarities between Sanskrit, Greek and Latin, which later resulted in the grouping of a number of languages as Indo-European languages. In 1793, he identified the Sandrokottos mentioned in Greek accounts as the Indian king Chandragupta Maurya, setting up a major milestone in the understanding of Indian history [3]. Jones passed away shortly after in 1794. His paper "On the Chronology of the Hindus" presents us with an excellent understanding of what was believed to be the history of India before India was colonized [2]. I will offer large extracts from the Jones essay to provide the context and the foundation for my analysis:

> *"The great antiquity of the Hindus is believed so firmly by themselves, and has been the subject of so much conversation among Europeans, that a short view of their chronological System, which has not yet been exhibited from certain authorities, may be acceptable to those who seek truth without partiality to received opinions, and without regarding any consequences that may result from their inquiries. The consequences, indeed, of truth cannot but*

be desirable, and no reasonable man will apprehend any danger to society from a general diffusion of its light; but we must not suffer ourselves to be dazzled by a false glare, nor mistake enigmas and allegories for historical verity. Attached to no system, and as much disposed to reject the Mosaic history, if it be proved erroneous, as to believe it, if it be confirmed by sound reasoning from indubitable evidence, I propose to lay before you a concise account of Indian Chronology, extracted from Sanskrit books, or collected from conversation with Pundits, ...

One of the most curious books in Sanscrit, and one of the oldest after the Vedas, is a tract on religious and civil duties, taken, as it is believed, from the oral instructions of Menu, son of Brahma, to the first inhabitants of the earth. An exceeding well collated copy of this most interesting law-tract is now before me; and I begin my dissertation with a few couplets from the first chapter of it:

> 'The sun causes the division of day and night, which are of two sorts, those of men and those of the Gods; the day, for the labour of all creatures in their several employments: the night for their slumber. A month is a day and night of the patriarchs; and it is divided into two parts; the bright half is their day for laborious exertions; the dark half, their night for sleep. A year is a day and night of the Gods; and that is also divided into two halves; the day is, when the sun moves toward the north; the night, when it moves toward the south. Learn now the duration of a night and day of Brahma with that of the ages respectively, and in order. Four thousand years of the Gods they call the Crita (or Satya) age; and its limits at the beginning and at the end are, in like manner, as many hundreds. In the three successive ages, together with their limits at the beginning and end of them are thousands and hundreds diminished by one. This aggregate of four ages, amounting to twelve thousand divine years, is called an age of the Gods; and a thousand such divine ages added together must be

> considered as a day of Brahma: his night has also the same duration. The before-mentioned age of the Gods, or twelve thousand of their years multiplied by seventy-one form what is named here below a Manwantara: There are alternate creations and destructions of worlds through innumerable Manwantaras: the Being supremely desirable, performs all this again and again.'

Such is the arrangement of infinite time, which the Hindus believe to have been revealed from Heaven, and which they generally understand in a literal sense: it seems to have intrinsic marks of being purely astronomical; … If we follow the analogy suggested by Menu, and suppose only a day and night to be called a year, we may divide the number of years in a divine age by three hundred and sixty, and the quotient will be twelve thousand, or the number of his divine years in one age: but, conjecture apart, we need only compare the two periods 4320000 and 25920, and we shall find, that among their common divisors, are 6, 9, 12, &c. 18, 36, 72, 144, &c.; which numbers with their several multiples, especially in a decuple progression, constitute some of the most celebrated periods of the Chaldeans, Greeks, Tartars, and even of the Indians. We cannot fail to observe, that the number 432, which appears to be the basis of the Indian system, is a 60th part of 25920, and, by continuing the comparison we might probably solve the whole enigma. … But, should it be thought improbable that the Indian astronomers in very early times had made more accurate observations than those of Alexandria, Bagdad, or Maraghah, and still more improbable that they should have relapsed with apparent cause into error, we may suppose that they formed their divine age by an arbitrary multiplication of 24000 by 180, according to Le Gentil, or of 21600 by 200, according to the comment on the Surya Siddhanta. Now as it is hardly possible that such coincidences should be accidental, we may hold it nearly demonstrated, that the period of a divine age was at first merely astronomical, and may consequently reject it from our present inquiry into the historical or civil chronology of India."

We can see from the above the working of Jones' keen mind. He was critically examining the information presented to him. Hindus at that time started their history from the very beginning of creation by Brahmā, but Jones figured out that the initial part of the story was really astronomical information couched as historical events. He also related these astronomical ages to the precession of the equinoxes, which is close to 25,920 years for one revolution. Jones continues:

> *"Let us, however, proceed to the avowed opinions of the Hindus, and see, when we have ascertained their system, whether we can reconcile it to the course of nature and the common sense of mankind. The aggregate of their four ages they call a divine age, and believe that, in every thousand such ages, or in every day of Brahma, fourteen Menus are successively invested by him with the sovereignty of the earth: each Menu, they suppose, transmits his empire to his sons and grandsons during a period of seventy-one divine ages; and such a period they name a Manwantara; but, since fourteen multiplied by seventy-one are not quite a thousand, we must conclude that six divine ages are allowed for intervals between the Manwantaras, or for the twilight of Brahma's day. Thirty such days, or Calpas, constitute, in their opinion, a month of Brahma; twelve such months, one of his years; and an hundred such years, his age; of which age they assert, that fifty years have elapsed. We are now then, according to the Hindus in the first day or Calpa of the first month of the fifty-first year of Brahma's age, and in the twenty-eighth divine age of the seventh Manwantara, of which divine age the three first human ages have passed, and four thousand eight hundred and eighty-eight of the fourth.*
>
> *In the present day of Brahma the first Menu was surnamed Swayambhuva, or son of the self-existent; and it is he by whom the institutes of religious and civil duties are supposed to have been delivered. In his time the Deity descended at a sacrifice, and, by his wife Satarupa, he had two, distinguished sons, and three daughters. This pair were created for the multiplication of the human species,*

after that new creation of the world which the Brahmans call Padmacalpiya, or the Lotos- creation.

If it were worth while to calculate the age of Menu's institutes, according to the Brahmans, we must multiply four million three hundred and twenty thousand by six times seventy-one, and add to the product the number of years already past in the seventh Manwantara. Of the five Menus who succeeded him, I have seen little more than the names; but the Hindu writings are very diffuse on the life and posterity of the seventh Menu, surnamed Vaivaswata, or Child of the Sun; he is supposed to have had ten sons, of whom the eldest was Icshwacu; and to have been accompanied by seven Rishis, or holy persons, whose names were, Casyapa, Atri, Vasishtha, Viswamitra, Gautama, Jamadagni, and Bharadwaja; ...

In the reign of this sun born monarch, the Hindus believe the whole earth to have been drowned, and the whole human race destroyed by a flood, except the pious prince himself, the seven Rishis, and their several wives; for they suppose his children to have been born after the deluge. This general pralaya, or destruction, is the subject of the first Purana, or sacred poem, which consists of fourteen thousand stanzas; and the story is concisely, but clearly and elegantly, told in the eighth book of the Bhagawata, from which I have abstracted the whole, and translated it with great care, but will only present you here with an abridgment of it.

> 'The demon Hayagriva having purloined the Vedas, from the custody of Brahma, while he was reposing at the close of the sixth Manwantara, the whole race of men became corrupt, except the seven Rishis and Satyavrata, who then reigned in Dravira, a maritime region to the south of Carnata: this prince was performing his ablutions in the river Critamala, when Vishnu appeared to him in the shape of a small fish, and, after several augmentations of bulk in different waters, was placed by Satyavrata in the ocean, where he thus addressed his

> amazed votary: "In seven days all creatures, who have offended me, shall be destroyed by a deluge, but thou shalt be secured in a capacious vessel miraculously formed: take therefore all kinds of medicinal herbs and esculent grain for food, and, together with the seven holy men, your respective wives, and pairs of all animals, enter the ark without fear; then shalt thou know God face to face, and all thy questions shall be answered." Saying this, he disappeared; and after seven days, the ocean began to overflow the coasts, and the earth to be flooded by constant showers, when Satyavrata, meditating on the Deity, saw a large vessel moving on the waters: he entered it, having in all respects conformed to the instructions of Vishnu; who, in the form of a vast fish, suffered the vessel to be tied with a great sea-serpent, as with a cable, to his measureless horn. When the deluge had ceased, Vishnu slew the demon, and recovered the Vedas, instructed Satyavrata in divine knowledge, and appointed him the seventh Menu by the name of Vaivaswata.'

Let us compare the two Indian accounts of the Creation and the Deluge with those delivered by Moses. It is not made a question in this tract, whether the first chapters of Genesis are to be understood in a literal, or merely in an allegorical sense; the only points before us are, whether the creation described by the first Menu, which the Brahmans called that of the Lotos, be not the same with that recorded in our Scripture; and whether the story of the seventh Menu be not one and the same with that of Noah. I propose the questions, but affirm nothing; leaving others to settle their opinions, whether Adam be derived from adim, which in Sanscrit means the first; or Menu from Nuh, the true name of the patriarch; whether the sacrifice, at which God is believed to have descended, alludes to the offering of Abel; and, on the whole, whether the two Menus can mean any other persons than the great progenitor, and the restorer of our species."

1.2 The Incarnations of Lord Viṣṇu

Jones then narrates the history as believed by Hindus with the description of ten incarnations of Lord Viṣṇu:

> *"On a supposition that Vaivaswata, or sun-born, was the Noah of Scripture, let us proceed to the Indian account of his posterity, which I extract from the Puranarthaprecasa, or The Puranas Explained: a work lately composed in Sanscrit by Radhacanta Sarman, a Pundit of extensive learning and great fame among the Hindus of this province. Before we examine the genealogies of kings, which he has collected from the Puranas, it will be necessary to give a general idea of the avataras, or descents, of the Deity. The Hindus believe innumerable such descents or special interpositions of Providence in the affairs of mankind, but they reckon ten principal avataras in the current period of four ages; and all of them are described, in order as they are supposed to occur, in the following Ode of Jayadeva, the great lyric poet of India.*
>
> *1. Thou recoverest the Veda in the water of the ocean of destruction, placing it joyfully in the bosom of an ark fabricated by thee, O Cesava, assuming the body of a fish. Be victorious, O Heri, lord of the universe!*
>
> *2. The earth stands firm on thy immensely broad back, which grows larger from the callus, occasioned by bearing that vast burden, O Cesava, assuming the body of a tortoise. Be victorious, O Heri, lord of the universe!*
>
> *3. The earth, placed on the point of thy tusk, remains fixed like the figure of a black antelope on the moon, O Cesava, assuming the form of a boar. Be victorious, O Heri, lord of the universe!*
>
> *4, The claw with a stupendous point, on the exquisite lotos of thy lion's paw, is the black bee that stung the body of the embowelled Hiranyacasipu, O Cesava, assuming the form of a man-lion. Be victorious, O Heri, lord of the universe!*

5. By thy power thou beguilest Bali, O thou miraculous dwarf, thou purifier of men with the water (of Ganga) springing from thy feet, O Cesava, assuming the form of a dwarf. Be victorious, O Heri, lord of the universe!

6. Thou bathest in pure water, consisting of the blood of Cshatriyas, the world, whose offences are removed, and who are relieved from the pain of other births, O Cesava, assuming the form of Parasurama. Be victorious, O Heri, lord of the universe!

7. With ease to thyself, with delight to the Genii of the eight regions, thou scatterest on all sides in the plain of combat the demon with ten heads, O Cesava, assuming the form of Rama Chambra. Be victorious, O Heri, lord of the universe!

8. Thou wearest on thy bright body a mantle shining like a blue cloud, or like the water of Yamuna tripping towards thee through fear of thy furrowing ploughshare, O Cesava, assuming the form of Balla Rama. Be victorious, O Heri, lord of the Universe!

9. Thou blamest (Oh, wonderful!) the whole Veda, when thou seest, O kind-hearted, the slaughter of cattle prescribed for sacrifice, O Cesava, assuming the body of Buddha. Be victorious, O Heri, lord of the universe!

10. For the destruction of all the impure, thou drawest thy cimeter like a blazing comet (how tremendous! O Cesava, assuming the body of Calci. Be victorious, O Heri, lord of the universe!"

1.3 The Position of Buddha

With the ninth incarnation of Lord Viṣṇu as Buddha, we arrive at a discernible historical setting. Sir William Jones next deliberated on the place of Buddha in the Hindu pantheon:

"These ten Avataras are by some arranged according to the thousands of divine years in each of the four ages, or in an arithmetical proportion from four to one; and, if such an arrangement were universally received, we should be able to

ascertain a very material point in the Hindu chronology; I mean the birth of Buddha, concerning which the different Pandits, whom I have consulted, and the same Pandits at different times have expressed a strange diversity of opinion. They all agree that Calci is yet to come, and that Buddha was the last considerable incarnation of the Deity; but the astronomers at Varanes place him in the third age, and Radhacant insists that he appeared after the thousandth year of the fourth. The learned and accurate author of the Dabistan, whose information concerning the Hindus is wonderfully correct, mentions an opinion of the Pandits, with whom he had conversed, that Buddha began his career ten years before the close of the third age; and Goverdhana of Cashmir, who had once informed me that Crishna, descended two centuries before Buddha, assured me lately that the Cashmirians admitted an interval of twenty-four years (others allow only twelve) between these two divine persons. The best authority, after all, is the Bhagawat itself, in the first chapter of which it is expressly declared, that "Buddha, the son of Jina, would appear at Cicata for the purpose of confounding the demons, just at "the beginning of the Caliyug." I have long been convinced, that, on these subjects, we can only reason satisfactorily from written evidence, and that our forensick rule must be invariably applied to take the declarations of the Brahmans most strongly against themselves; that is, against their pretentious to antiquity; so that, on the whole, we may safely place Buddha just at the beginning of the present age: but what is the beginning of it? When this question was proposed to Radhacant, he answered, "Of a period comprising more than four hundred thousand years, "the first two or three thousand may reasonably be called the beginning." On my demanding written evidence, he produced a book of some authority, composed by a learned Goswami, and entitled Bhagawatamarita, or the Nectar of the Bhagawat, on which it is a metrical comment; and the couplet which he read from it deserves to be cited. After the just mentioned account of Buddha in the text, the commentator says,

> 'He became visible, the-thousand-and-second-year-of-the-Cali-age being past; his body of-a-colour-between-white and-ruddy, with two-arms, without-hair on his head.'

Cicata, named in the text as the birth-place of Buddha, the Goswami supposes to have been Dhermaranya, a wood near Gaya, where a colossal image of that ancient deity still remains. It seemed to me of black stone: but, as I saw it by torch-light, I cannot be positive as to its colour, which may indeed have been changed by time.

The Brahmans universally speak of the Bauddhas with all the malignity of an intolerant spirit; yet the most orthodox among them consider Buddha himself as an incarnation of Vishnu. This is a contradiction hard to be reconciled, unless we cut the knot, instead of untying it, by supposing with Giorgi, that there were two Buddhas, the younger of whom established the new religion, which gave so great offence in India, and was introduced into China in the first century of our era. The Cashmirian before mentioned asserted this fact, without being led to it by any question that implied it; and we may have reason to suppose that Buddha is in truth only a general word for a Philosopher. The author of a celebrated Sanscrit Dictionary, entitled from his name Amaracosha, who was himself a Bauddha, and flourished in the first century before Christ, begins his vocabulary with nine words that signify heaven, and proceeds to those which mean a deity in general; after which come different classes of Gods, Demigods, and Demons, all by generic names; and they are followed by two very remarkable heads; first (not the general names of Buddha, but) the names of a Buddha-in-general of which he gives us eighteen, such as Muni, Sastri, Munindra, Vinayaca, Samantabhadra, Dhermaraja; Sugata, and the like; most of them significative of excellence, wisdom, virtue, and sanctity; secondly, the names of a particular-Buddha-Muni-who-descended-in-the-family-of-Sacya (these are the very words of the original) and his titles are, Sacyamuni, Sacyasinha, Servarthasiddha, Saudhodani,

Gautama, Arcabandhu, or Kinsman of the Sun, and Mayadevisuta, or Child of Maya. Thence the author passes to the different epithets of particular Hindu deities. When I pointed out this curious passage to Radhacant, he contended that the first eighteen names were general epithets, and the following seven proper names, or patronymics, of one of the same person; but Ramalochan, my own teacher, who though not a Brahman, is an excellent scholar and a very sensible unprejudiced man, assured me that Buddha was a generic word, like Deva, and that the learned author, having exhibited the names of a Devata in general, proceeded to those of a Buddha in general, before he came to particulars: he added, that Buddha might mean a Sage or Philosopher, though Buddha was the word commonly used for a mere wise man without supernatural powers. It seems highly probable, on the whole, that the Buddha, whom Jayadeva celebrates in his Hymn, was the Sacyasinha, or Lion Sacya, who, though he forbade the sacrifices of cattle, which the Vedas enjoin, was believed to be Vishnu himself in a human form, and that another Buddha, one perhaps of his followers in a later age, assuming his name and character, attempted to overset the whole system of the Brahnmans, and was the cause of that persecution, from which the Bauddhas are known to have fled into very distant regions. May we not reconcile the singular difference of opinion among the Hindus as to the time of Buddha's appearance, by supposing that they have confounded the two Buddhas, the first of whom was born a few years before the close of the last age, and the second, when above a thousand years of the present age had elapsed? We know from better authorities, and with as much certainty as can justly be expected on so doubtful a subject, the real time, compared with our own era, when the ancient Buddha began to distinguish himself; and it is for this reason principally that I have dwelt with minute anxiety on the subject of the last Avatar."

This is followed by a discussion on the dating of Buddha with dates varying from 1366 BCE to 959 BCE for his birth:

"The Brahmans, who assisted Abulfazl in his curious but superficial account of his master's empire, informed him, if the figures in the Ayini Acbari be correctly written, that a period of 2962 years had elapsed from the birth of Buddha to the 40th year of Acbar's reign; which computation will place his birth in the 1366th year before that of our Saviour; but, when the Chinese government admitted a new religion from India in the first century of our era, they made particular enquiries concerning the age of the old Indian Buddha, whose birth, according to Couplet, they place in the 41st year of their 28th cycle, or 1036 years before Christ; and they call him, says he, Foe, the son of Moye, or Maya; but M. De Guignes, on the authority of four Chinese historians asserts, that Fo was born about the year before Christ 1027, in the kingdom of Cashmir. Giorgi, or rather Cassiano, from whose papers his work was compiled, assures us, that, by the calculation of the Tibetians, he appeared only 959 years before the Christian epoch; and M. Bailly, with some hesitation, places him 1031 before it, but inclines to think him far more ancient, confounding him, as I have done in a former tract, with the first Buddha, or Mercury, whom the Goths called Woden, and of whom I shall presently take particular notice. Now, whether we assume the medium of the four last-mentioned dates, or implicitly rely on the authorities quoted by De Guignes, we may conclude, that Buddha was first distinguished in this country about a thousand years before the beginning of our era; and whoever, in so early an age, expects a certain epoch unqualified with about or nearly, will be greatly disappointed. Hence it is clear, that, whether the fourth age of, the Hindus began about one thousand years before Christ, according to Goverdhan's account of Buddha's birth, or two thousand, according to that of Radhacant, the common opinion that 4888 years of it are now elapsed, is erroneous; and here for the present we leave Buddha, with an intention of returning to him in due time; observing only, that if the learned Indians differ so widely in their accounts of the age, when their ninth Avatar appeared in their country, we may be assured that they have no certain

chronology before him, and may suspect the certainty of all the relations concerning even his appearance. ..."

We see here that Jones was confused between Budha (Mercury) and Buddha.

1.4 The Solar and Lunar Races

Jones next discussed the Solar and Lunar races:

"From this Menu the whole race of men is believed to have descended; for the seven Rishis, who were preserved with him in the ark, are not mentioned as fathers of human families; but, since his daughter Ila was married, as the Indians tell us, to the first Buddha, or Mercury, the son of Chandra, or the Moon, a male-deity, whose father was Atri, son of Brahma, (where again we meet with an allegory purely astronomical or poetical) his posterity are divided into two great branches, called the Children of the Sun, from his own supposed father, and, the Children of the Moon, from the parent of his daughter's husband. The lineal male descendants in both these families are supposed to have reigned in the cities of Ayodhya, or Audh, and Pratishthana, or Vitora, respectively till the thousandth year of the present age, and the names of all the princes in both lines having been diligently collected by Radhacant from several Puranas, I exhibit them in two columns, arranged by myself with great attention. (Note: Rearranged in series by the author.)

SECOND AGE.

CHILDREN OF THE SUN:

1. Icshwacu, 2. Vicucshi, 3. Cucutstha, 4. Aneas, 5. Prithu, 6. Viswagandhi, 7. Chandra, 8. Yuvanaswa, 9. Srava, 10. Vrihadaswa, 11. Dhundhumara, 12. Dridhaswa, 13. Heryaswa, 14. Nicumbha, 15. Crisaswa, 16. Senajit, 17. Yuvanaswa, 18. Mandhatri, 19. Purucutsa, 20. Trasadasyu, 21. Anaranya, 22. Heryaswa, 23. Praruna, 24. Trivindhana, 25. Satyavrata, 26. Trisancu, 27. Harischandra, 28. Rohita, 29. Harita, 30. Champa,

31. Sudeva, 32. Vijaya, 33. Bharuca, 34. Vrica, 35. Bahuca, 36. Sagara, 37. Asamanjas, 38. Ansumat, 39. Bhagiratha, 40. Sruta, 41. Nabha, 42. Sindhudwipa, 43. Ayutayush, 44. Ritaperna, 45. Saudasa, 46. Asmaca, 47. Mulaca, 48. Dasaratha, 49. Aidabidi, 50. Viswasaha, 51. Chatwanga, 52. Dirghabahu, 53. Raghu, 54. Aja, 55. Dasaratha, 56. Rama.

CHILDREN OF THE MOON:

1. Budha, 2. Puraravas, 3. Ayush, 4. Nabusha, 5. Yayati, 6. Puru, 7. Janamejaya, 8. Prachinwat, 9. Pravira, 10. Menasyu, 11. Charupada, 12. Sudyu, 13. Bahugava, 14. Sanyati, 15. Ahanyati, 16. Raudraswa, 17. Riteyush, 18. Rantinava, 19. Sumati, 20. Aiti, 21. Dushmanta, 22. Bharata, 23. Vitatha, 24. Manyu, 25. Vrihatcshetra, 26. Hastin, 27. Ajamidha, 28. Ricsha, 29. Samwarana, 30. Curu, 31. Jahnu, 32. Suratha, 33. Viduratha, 34. Sarvabhauma, 35. Viswasaha Jayatsena, 36. Radhica, 37. Ayutayush, 38. Acrodhana, 39. Devatithi, 40. Ricsha, 41. Dilipa, 42. Pratipa, 43. Santanu, 44. Vichitravirya, 45. Pandu, 46. Yudhishthir.

It is agreed among all the Pundits, that Rama, their seventh incarnate Divinity, appeared as king of Ayodhya in the interval between the silver and the brazen ages; and, if we suppose him to have began his reign at the very beginning of that interval, still three thousand three hundred years of the Gods, or a million one hundred and eighty-eight thousand lunar years of mortals, will remain in the silver age, during which the fifty-five princes between Vaivaswata and Rama must have governed the world; but, reckoning thirty years for a generation, which is rather too much for a long succession of eldest sons, as they are said to have been, we cannot, by the course of nature, extend the second age of the Hindus beyond sixteen hundred and fifty solar years. If we suppose them not to have been eldest sons, and even to have lived longer than modern princes in a dissolate age, we shall find only a period of two thousand years; and, if we remove the difficulty by admitting miracles, we must cease to reason, and may as well believe at once whatever the Brahmans chuse to tell us.

In the lunar pedigree we meet with another absurdity equally fatal to the credit of the Hindu system. As far as the twenty-second degree of descent from Vaivaswata, the synchronism of the two families appears tolerably regular, except that the Children of the Moon were not all eldest sons; for king Yayati appointed the youngest of his five sons to succeed him in India, and allotted inferior kingdoms to the other four, who had offended him; part of the dacshin, or the south, to Yadu, the ancestor of Crishna; the north to Anu, the east to Druhya, and the west to Turvasu, from whom the Pandits believe, or pretend to believe, in compliment to our nation, that we are descended. But of the subsequent degrees in the lunar line they know so little, that, unable to supply a considerable interval between Bharat and Vitatha, whom they call son and successor, and are under a necessity of asserting, that the great ancestor of Yudhishthir actually reigned seven and twenty thousand years: a fable of the same class with that of his wonderful birth, which is the subject of a beautiful Indian drama. Now, if we suppose his life to have lasted no longer than that of other mortals, and admit Vitatha and the rest to have been his regular successors, we shall fall into another absurdity; for then, if the generations in both lines were nearly equal, as they would naturally have been, we shall find Yudhishthir, who reigned confessedly at the close of the brazen age, nine generations older than Rama, before whose birth the silver age is allowed to have ended. After the name of Bharat, therefore, I have set an asterisk, to denote a considerable chasm in the Indian history, and have inserted between brackets, as out of their places, his twenty-four successors, who reigned, if at all, in the following age, immediately before the war of the Mahabharat. The fourth Avatar, which is placed in the interval between the first and second ages, and the fifth which soon followed it, appear to be moral fables, grounded on historical facts. The fourth was the punishment of an impious monarch, by the Deity himself bursting from a marble column, in the shape of a lion; and the fifth was the humiliation of an arrogant prince, by so contemptible an agent as a mendicant dwarf. After these, and immediately before Buddha, come three great warriors, all named Rama; but it may justly be made a question, whether they are not three representations of one person, or three different ways of relating the same history. The first and second Ramas are said to have been contemporary; or whether all or any of them mean Rama, the son of Cush, I leave others to determine. The mother of the second Rama was named Caushalya, which is a derivative of Cushala, and, though his father be distinguished by the title or epithet of Dasaratha, signifying that his car-chariot bore him to all quarters of the world; yet the name of Cush, as the Cashmirians pronounce it, is preserved entire in that of his son and successor, and shadowed in that of his ancestor Vicucshi; nor can a just objection be made to this opinion from the nasal Arabian vowel in the Ramah, mentioned by Moses, since the very word Arab begins with the same letter, which the Greeks and Indians could not pronounce; and they were obliged, therefore to express it by the vowel which most resembled it. On this question, however, I assert nothing; nor on another, which might be proposed: "Whether the fourth and fifth Avatars be not allegorical stories of the two presumptuous monarchs, Nimrod and Belus!" The hypothesis, that government was first established, laws enacted, and agriculture encouraged in India by Rama about three thousand eight hundred years ago, agrees with the received account of Noah's death, and the previous settlement of his immediate descendants. (Note: Rearranged in series by the author. Jones makes the first king of Lunar dynasty the contemporary of sixth king of Solar dynasty.)

THIRD AGE.

CHILDREN OF THE SUN:

1. Cusha, 2. Atithi, 3. Nishadha, 4. Nabhas, 5. Pundarica, 6. Cshemadhanwas, 7. Devanica, 8. Ahinagu, 9. Paripatra, 10. Ranachhala, 11. Vajranabha, 12. Arca, 13. Sugana, 14. Vidhriti,

15. Hiranyanabha, 16. Pushya, 17. Dhruvasandhi, 18. Sudersana, 19. Agniverna, 20. Sighra, 21. Maru, supposed to be still alive, 22. Prasusruta, 23. Sandhi, 24. Amersana, 25. Mahaswat, 26. Viswabhahu, 27. Prasenajit, 28. Tacshaca, 29. Vrihadbala, 30. Vrihadrana (Y.B.C. 3100).

CHILDREN OF THE MOON:

1. Vitatha, 2. Manyu 3. Vrihatcshetra 4. Hastin, 5. Ajamidha, 6. Ricsha, 7. Samwarana, 8. Curu, 9. Jahnu, 10. Suratha, 11. Viduratha, 12. Sarvabhauma, 13. Jayatsena, 14. Radhica, 15. Ayutayush, 16. Acrodhana, 17. Devatithi, 18. Ricsha, 19. Dilipa, 20. Pratipa, 21. Santanu, 22. Vichitravirya, 23. Pandu, 24. Yudhishthir 25. Paricshit.

Here we have only nine and twenty princes of the solar line between Rama and Vrihadrana exclusively; and their reigns, during the whole brazen age, are supposed to have lasted near eight hundred and sixty-four thousand years: a supposition evidently against nature, the uniform course of which allows only a period of eight hundred and seventy, or, at the very utmost, of a thousand years, for twenty-nine generations. Paricshit, the great nephew and successor of Yudhishthir, who had recovered the throne from Duryodhan, is allowed without controversy to have reigned in the interval between the brazen and earthen ages, and to have died at the setting in of the Caliyug; so that, if the Pandits of Cashmir and Varanes have made a right calculation of Buddha's appearance, the present, or fourth, age must have begun about a thousand years before the birth of Christ, and consequently the reign of Icshwacu could not have been earlier than four thousand years before that great epoch; and even that date will, perhaps, appear, when it shall be strictly examined, to be near two thousand years earlier than the truth. I cannot leave the third Indian age, in which the virtues and vices of mankind are said to have been equal, without observing, that even the close of it is manifestly fabulous and poetical, with hardly more appearance of historical truth than the tale of Troy, or of the

Argonauts; for Yudhishthir, it seems, was the son of Dherma, the Genius of Justice; Bhima of Pavan, or the God of Wind; Arjun of Indra, or the Firmament; Nacul and Sahadeva, of the two Cumars, the Castor and Pollux of India; and Bhishma, their reputed great uncle, was the child of Ganga, or the Ganges, by Santanu, whose brother Devapi is supposed to be still alive in the city of Calapa; all which fictions may be charming embellishments of an heroic poem, but are just as absurd in civil history as the descent of the two royal families from the Sun and the Moon. (Note: Rearranged in series by the author.)

FOURTH AGE.

CHILDREN OF THE SUN:

1. Urucriya, 2. Vatsavriddha, 3. Prativyoma, 4. Bhanu, 5. Devaca, 6. Sahadeva, 7. Vira, 8. Vrihadaswa, 9. Bhanumat, 10. Praticaswa, 11. Supratica, 12. Marudeva 13. Sunacshatra, 14. Pushcara, 15. Antaricsha, 16. Sutapas, 17. Amitrajit, 18. Vrihadraja, 19. Barhi, 20. Critanjaya, 21. Rananjaya, 22. Sanjaya, 23. Slocya, 24. Suddhoda, 25. Langalada, 26. Prasenajit, 27. Cshudraca, 28. Sumitra (Y. B. C. 2100).

CHILDREN OF THE MOON:

1. Janamejaya, 2. Satanica, 3. Sahasranica, 4. Aswamedhaja, 5. Asimacrishna, 6. Nemichacra, 7. Upta, 8. Chitraratha, 9. Suchiratha, 10. Dhritimat, 11. Sushena, 12. Sunitha, 13. Nrichacshuh, 14. Suchinala, 15. Pariplava, 16. Sunaya, 17. Medhavin, 18. Nripanjaya, 19. Derva, 20. Timi, 21. Vrihadratha, 22. Sudasa, 23. Satanica, 24. Durmadana, 25. Rahinara, 26. Dandapani, 27. Nimi, 28. Cshemaca.

In both families, we see, thirty generations are reckoned from Yudhishthir, and from Vrihadbala his contemporary (who was killed in the war of Bharat by Abhimanyu, son of Arjun and father of Paricshit) to the time when the solar and lunar dynasties are believed to have become extinct in the present divine age; and for these generations the Hindus allot a period of one thousand years only, or a hundred years for three generations; which calculation, though probably too large, is yet moderate enough, compared with their absurd accounts of the preceding ages; but they reckon exactly the same number of years for twenty generations only in the family of Jarasandha, whose son was contemporary with Yudhishthir, and founded a new dynasty of princes in Magadha, or Bahar; and this exact coincidence of the times, in which the three races are supposed to have been extinct, has the appearance of an artificial chronology, formed rather from imagination than from historical evidence, especially as twenty kings, in an age comparatively modern, could not have reigned a thousand years. I, nevertheless, exhibit the list of them as a curiosity, but am far from being convinced that all of them ever existed; that, if they did exist, they could not have reigned more than seven hundred years. I am fully persuaded by the course of nature and the concurrent opinion of mankind.

Kings of Magadha.

1. Sahadeva, 2. Marjari, 3. Srutasravas, 4. Ayutayush, 5. Niramitra, 6. Sunacshatra, 7. Vrihetsena, 8. ar majit, 9. Srutanjaya, 10. Vipra, 11. Suchi, 12. Cshema, 13. Suvrata, 14. Dhermasutra, 15. Srama, 16. Dridhasena, 17. Sumati, 18. Subala 19. Sunita, 20. Satyajit.

Puranjaya, son of the twentieth king, was put to death by his minister, Sunaca, who placed his own son Pradyota on the throne of his master; and this revolution constitutes an epoch of the highest importance in our present enquiry; first, because it happened according to the Bhagawatamrita, two years exactly before Buddha's appearance in the same kingdom: next, because it is believed by the Hindus to have taken place three thousand eight hundred and eighty-eight years ago, or two thousand one hundred years before Christ; and lastly, because a regular chronology, according to the number of years in each dynasty, has been established from the accession of Pradyota to the subversion of the genuine Hindu government; and that chronology I will now lay before you, after observing only, that Radhacant himself says nothing of Buddha in this part of his work, though he particularly mentions the two preceding Avataras in their proper places."

1.5 The Rise of Magadha

Jones then continues with the list of the kings of Magadha. The chronology though is very different as it was not yet synchronized with European chronology.

"Kings of Magadha.

1. Pradyota (Y. B. C. 2100), 2. Palace, 3. Visachayupa, 4. Rajaca, 5. Nandiverdhana (5 reigns = 138 years.), 6. Sisunaga (Y. B. C. 1962), 7. Cacaverna, 8. Cshemadherman, 9. Cshetrajnya, 10. Vidhisara, 11. Ajatasatru, 12. Darbhaca, 13. Ajaya, 14. Nandiverdhana, 15. Mahanandi, (10 reigns = 360 y.), 16. Nanda (Y. B. C. 1602).

This prince, of whom frequent mention is made in the Sanscrit books, is said to have been murdered, after a reign of a hundred years, by a very learned and ingenious, but passionate and vindictive, Brahman, whose name was Chanacya, and who raised to the throne a man of the Maurya race, named Chandragupta. By the death of Nanda, and his sons, the Cshatriya family of Pradyota became extinct.

Maurya Kings.

1. Chandragupta (Y. B. C. 1502), 2. Varisara, 3. Asocaverdhana, 4. Suyasas, 5. Desaratha, 6. Sangata, 7. Salisuca, 8. Somasarman, 9. Satadhanwas, 10. Vrihadratha (10 reigns = 137 y.)

On the death of the tenth Maurya king, his place was assumed by his commander in chief, Pushpamitra.

Sunga Kings.

1. Pushpamitra (Y. B. C. 1365), 2. Agnimitra, 3. Sujyeshtha, 4. Vasumitra, 5. Abhadraca, 6. Pulinda, 7. Ghosha, 8. Vajramitra, 9. Bhagavata, 10. Devabhuti (10 r. = 112 y.)

The last prince was killed by his minister Vasudeva, of the Canna race, who usurped the throne of Magadha.

Canna Kings.

1. Vasudeva, 2. Bhumitra, 3. Narayana, 4. Susarman (4 reigns = 345 y.)"

The power then shifted to Āndhras, but the Purāṇas seem to indicate that the Āndhra kings were ruling Magadha, which was highly unlikely and may be due to some confusion:

"A Sudra, of the Andhra family, having murdered his master Susarman, and seized the government, founded a new dynasty of

Andhra Kings.

1. Balin (Y. B. C. 908), 2. Crishna, 3. Srisantacarna, 4. Paurnamasa, 5. Lambodara, 6. Vivilaca, 7. Meghaswata, 8. Vatamana, 9. Talaca, 10. Sivaswati, 11. Purishhabheru, 12. Sunandana, 13. Chacoraca, 14. Bataca, 15. Gomatin, 16. Purimat, 17. Medasiras, 18. Sirascandha, 19. Yajnyasri, 20. Vijaya, 21. Chandrabija (21 reigns= 456 y.).

After the death of Chandrabija, which happened, according to the Hindus, 396 years before Vicramaditya, or 452 B. C. we hear no more of Magadha as an independent kingdom; but Radhacant has exhibited the names of seven dynasties, in which seventy-six princes are said to have reigned one thousand three hundred and ninety-nine years in Avabhriti, a town of the Dacshin, or South, which we commonly call Decan. The names of the seven dynasties, or of the families who established them, are Abhira, Gardabhin, Canca, Yavana, Turushcara, Bhurunda, Maula; of which the Yavanas are by some, not generally, supposed to have been Ionians or Greeks, but the Turushcaras and Maulas are universally believed to have been Turcs and Moguls; yet Radhacant adds, "when "the Maula race was extinct, five princes, named Bhunanda Bangira, Sisunandi, Yasonandi, and Praviraca, reigned an hundred and six years (or till the year 1053 in the city of Cilacila," which he tells me, he understands to be in the country of the Maharashtras, or Mahrattas, and here ends his Indian chronology; for "after Praviraca," says he, "this empire was divided among Mlechhas, or Infidels." This account of the seven 'modern dynasties appears very doubtful in itself, and has no relation to our present inquiry; for their dominion seems confined to the Decan, without extending to Magadha; nor have we any reason to believe that a race of Grecian princes ever established a kingdom in either of those countries. As to the Moguls, their dynasty still subsists, at least nominally, unless that of Chengiz be meant; and his successors could not have reigned in any part of India for the period of three hundred years, which is assigned to the Maulas; nor is it probable that the word Turc, which an Indian could have easily pronounced and clearly expressed in the Nagari letters, should have been corrupted into Turushcara. On the whole, we may safely close the most authentic system of Hindu Chronology that I have yet been able to procure, with the death of Chandrabija."

1.6 The Inquiring Mind

After presenting the information gathered from traditional sources, Jones analyzed it and offered the revised Hindu chronology as follows:

"Should any farther information be attainable, we shall, perhaps, in due time attain it either from books or inscriptions in the Sanscrit language; but from the materials with which we are at present supplied, we may establish as indubitable the two following propositions: That the three first ages of the Hindus are chiefly mythological, whether their mythology was founded on the dark

enigmas of their astronomers; or on the heroic fictions of their poets; and that the fourth, or historical age, cannot be carried farther back than about two thousand years before Christ. Even in the history of the present age, the generations of men and the reigns of kings are extended beyond the course of nature, and beyond the average resulting from the accounts of the Brahmans themselves; for they assign to an hundred and forty two modern reigns a period of three thousand one hundred and fifty-three years, or about twenty-two years to a reign one with another; yet they represent only four Canna princes on the throne of Magadha for a period of three hundred and forty-five years; now it is even more improbable that four successive kings should have reigned eighty-six years and three months each, than that Nanda, should have been king a hundred years, and murdered at last. Neither account can be credited; but, that we may allow the highest probable antiquity to the Hindu government, let us grant that three generations of men were equal on an average to an hundred years, and that Indian princes have reigned, one with another, two-and-twenty: then reckoning thirty generations from Arjun, the brother of Yudhisthira, to the extinction of his race, and taking the Chinese account of Buddha's birth from M. De Guignes, as the most authentic medium between Abulfazl and the Tibetians, we may arrange the corrected Hindu Chronology according to the following table, supplying the word about or nearly (since perfect accuracy cannot, be obtained, and ought not to be required) before every date. (Note: Rearranged in series by the author.)

1. Abhimanyu, son of Arjun (Y.B.C. 2029), 2. Pradyota (Y.B.C. 1029), 3. Buddha (Y.B.C. 1027), 4. Nanda (Y.B.C. 699), 5. Balin (Y.B.C. 149), 6. Vicramaditya (Y.B.C. 56), 7. Devapala, king of Gaur (Y.B.C. 23).

If we take the date of Buddha's appearance from Abulfazl, we must place Abhimanyu 2368 years before Christ, unless we calculate from the twenty kings of Magadha, and allow seven hundred years, instead of a thousand, between Arjun and Pradyota, which will bring us again very nearly to the date exhibited in the table; and, perhaps, we can hardly approach nearer to the truth. As to Raja Nanda, if he really sat on the throne a whole century, we must bring down the Andhra dynasty to the age of Vicrumaditya, who with his feudatories had probably obtained so much power during the reign of those princes, that they had little more than a nominal sovereignty, which ended with Chandrabija in the third or fourth century of the Christian era; having, no doubt, been long reduced to insignificance by the kings of Gaur, descended from Gopala. But, if the author of the Dabistan be warranted in fixing the birth of Buddha ten years before the Caliyug, we must thus correct the Chronological Table: (Note: Rearranged in series by the author.)

1. Buddha (Y. B. C. 1027), 2. Paricshit (Y. B. C. 1017), 3. Pradyota (reckoning 20 or 30 Generations, Y. B. C. 317 or 17), 4. Nanda (Y.A.C. 13 or 313).

This correction would oblige us to place Vicramaditya before Nanda, to whom, as all the Pundits agree, he was long posterior and if this be an historical fact, it seems to confirm the Bhagawatamrita, which fixes the beginning of the Culiyug about a thousand years before Buddha; besides that Balin would then be brought down at least to the sixth, and Chundrabija to the tenth century after Christ, without leaving room for the subsequent dynasties, if they reigned successively.

Thus have we given a sketch of Indian history through the longest period fairly assignable to it, and have traced the foundation of the Indian empire above three thousand eight hundred years from the present time; but, on a subject in itself so obscure, and so much clouded by the fictions of the Brahmans, who, to aggrandize themselves, have designedly raised their antiquity beyond the truth, we must be satisfied with probable conjecture and just reasoning from the best attainable data; nor can we hope for a system of Indian Chronology, to which no objection can be made, unless the astronomical books in Sanscrit shall clearly ascertain the places of the colures in some precise years of the historical age, not by loose traditions, like that of a coarse observation by Chiron, who possibly never existed (for "he lived," says Newton, "in the golden age," which must long have preceded the Argonautic expedition) but by such evidence as our own astronomers and scholars shall allow to be unexceptionable.

A CHRONOLOGICAL TABLE,
according to one of the Hypotheses intimated in the preceding Tract.

Christian and Muselman	*Hindu*	*Years from 1788 of our era*
Adam	*Menu I. Age I.*	*5794*
Noah	*Menu II.*	*4737*
Deluge		*4138*
Nimrod	*Hiranyacasipu. Age II.*	*4006*
Bel	*Bali*	*3892*
Rama	*Rama. Age III.*	*3187*
Noah's death		*3787*
	Pradyota	*2817*
	Buddha. Age IV.	*2815*
	Nanda	*2487*
	Balin	*1937*
	Vicramaditya	*1844*
	Devapala	*1811*
Christ		*1787*
	Narayanpala	*1721*
	Saca	*1709*
Walid		*1080*
Mahmud		*786*
Chengiz		*548*
Taimur		*391*
Babur		*276*
Nadirshah		*49"*

I have quoted extensively from the brilliant paper by Sir William Jones. He arrived at the dates calculating backward from the writing of his paper in 1788. I have selected some historical people of interest from the Table above and converted the dates to the Common Era as shown below:

1. Pradyota (1030 BCE); 2. Buddha (1028 BCE); 3. Nanda (700 BCE); 4. Balin (150 BCE); 5. Vikramāditya (57 BCE); 6. Devapāla (24 BCE); 7. Nārāyaṇapāla (66 CE); and 8. Śaka (78 CE).

The major surprise here is that when Jones began his inquiry, it was believed that Devapāla ruled in 24 BCE, while Nārayaṇapāla ruled in 66 CE. Modern historians place them in the ninth/tenth century CE in Bengal. This is a huge gap that is worth pointing out. In the Bādal pillar inscription, Devapāla claims to have vanquished the Hūṇas [4], but having Hūṇas in ninth century CE is problematic. Muslims were already at the frontiers of India in seventh century CE. Hūṇas did form a small principality known as Hūṇa Maṇḍala after their defeat at the hands of Hindu kings, but whether they could have retained their identity for so long after their defeat in sixth century CE is worth looking into.

Now that we know the history as believed by Hindus at the beginning of colonial rule, it is time to review the current version of Indian history and see how a starkly different history of India has emerged based on two centuries of intensive research since then.

Notes:

1. The Life of Swami Vivekananda (1960): 213-214
2. Jones (1807). Article was written in January 1788.
3. Jones (1793).
4. Ganguli (1994): 46.

"It is not because the truth is too difficult to see that we make mistakes. ... We make mistakes because the easiest and most comfortable course for us is to seek insight where it accords with our emotions - especially selfish ones."

- Aleksandr Solzhenitsyn

2. THE OFFICIAL STORY

The framework of the modern history of India was developed by European scholars during the time India was under British Rule. There are two sheet anchors of Indian history, based on which the chronology of Indian history has been derived. These two sheet anchors are the identification of Sandrokottos of Greek accounts with Chandragupta Maurya, and the identification of Devānāmpriya Priyadarśī, who has mentioned a number of Greek kings in his inscriptions, with Aśoka Maurya, grandson of Chandragupta Maurya. With these two sheet anchors in place, the chronology of Indian history was developed by working backward and forward in time from the assumed dates of Chandragupta Maurya and Aśoka Maurya. These two synchronisms will be investigated in depth in this book to show that these synchronisms are not as strong as they are made out to be.

For now, I will briefly present the official chronological history of India that was developed over the past two centuries starting with the identification of Sandrokottos with Chandragupta Maurya by Sir William Jones in 1793 CE [1], a few years after his publication of the traditional history of India discussed in the previous chapter. This is the chronology that is taught all over the world as representing the true history of India based on all available evidence. It is summarized here in order to compare it with the alternative chronology proposed in this book and to show that the available evidence has been twisted/forced to fit this official chronology. A number of books have been consulted for general chronological summary [2-6]. Exact references are provided for specific dates. I will start the chronological summary with the Indus Valley Civilization (IVC), as the formative years of the Indian civilization prior to IVC starting from Mehrgarh are not subject to controversy.

2.1 Indus Valley Civilization

Indus Valley Civilization developed along the banks of the Indus river and covered the area of modern Pakistan, Northwest India and modern Gujarat. The formative years of IVC can be dated to around 3000 BCE. The mature phase of this civilization lasted between 2600-1900 BCE. IVC was essentially pre-Vedic as well as non-Vedic. The cities were well planned. The people used a script that is still not deciphered. They used bricks which had a ratio of 1:2:4 for height to width to length. The bricks with the same ratios are still used all over India. This civilization started its decline around 1900 BCE and ceased to exist by about 1700 BCE.

2.2 The Vedic Age

Around 1700 BCE a group of nomadic people started arriving in India. This migration gathered momentum around 1400 BCE with the arrival of Aryans, who brought early portions of the Vedas with them. Between 1700-1400 BCE, two groups of Aryans, Indo-Aryans and Iranian Aryans collectively called Indo-Iranians, lived together in Eastern Iran and Afghanistan. Indo-Aryans crossed the Indus into the Indian sub-continent around 1400 BCE. Here they vanquished the indigenous people, who were called by pejorative names such as Dāsa (slave or servant) and Dasyu (enemy or impious man). They lived in the region of Punjab for about five centuries and completed composing the Ṛgveda. Then they moved to the middle country or Madhyadeśa around 900 BCE. Madhyadeśa was the region between the rivers Saraswatī and Ganga/Ganges. By 600 BCE, the entire Gangetic basin was colonized by the Aryans.

2.3 The Rise of Magadha

Around 600 BCE, the Indian peninsula consisted of sixteen kingdoms and republics known as Mahājanapadas. For more than a thousand years till the beginning of the sixth century CE, the Mahājanapada of Magadha was the centre of political activity. The Mahājanapada of Magadha, starting from the current day Patna and Gaya districts, developed into mighty empires comprising most of North India. Initially Rājagṛha (current day Rajgir) was the capital city of Magadha, which was later shifted to Pāṭaliputra (current day Patna). Magadha started its military conquest under Bimbisāra by conquering the neighboring kingdom of Aṅga, whose capital Champā was one of the six major cities of the time. This was followed by the peaceful acquisition of Kāśī. Ajātaśatru, son of Bimbisāra, continued the military conquest of neighboring Mahājanapadas. The reigns of Bimbisāra and Ajātaśatru saw the rise of two important religions: Buddhism and Jainism. About 100 years after Ajātaśatru, Nanda kings became the rulers of Magadha. The last Nanda king was ruling North India when Alexander the Great invaded India. He has been called Agrammes or Xandrames by Greek writers. Accepted dates of the Buddha and Mahāvīra along with the kings of Magadha are listed below in Table 2.1.

Table 2.1: Magadha before Mauryas [7]

Buddha	567-487 BCE
Mahāvīra	539-467 BCE
Bimbisāra	544-493 BCE
Ajātaśatru	493-462 BCE
Next four kings	462-430 BCE
Śiśunāga and successors	430-364 BCE
Nanda kings	364-324 BCE

2.4 Encounter with the Greeks

Chandragupta Maurya ascended the throne after deposing the last Nanda ruler with the help of a Brāhmaṇa Chāṇakya, who became his prime minister. Chandragupta Maurya is referred to as Sandrokottos in Greek accounts. The identification of Sandrokottos with Chandragupta Maurya forms the first sheet anchor of Indian chronology. After Alexander's death, Seleucus Nikator became the ruler of part of Alexander's empire, which included Syria and most of Asia Minor. Around 305 BCE, Seleucus attacked India, but was defeated by Chandragupta Maurya. Seleucus retreated after giving his daughter in marriage to Chandragupta.

The grandson of Chandragupta was Aśoka Maurya, who accepted Buddhism after the bloody Kaliṅga War. He called himself Devānāmpriya Priyadarśī in his inscriptions and mentioned five Greek kings to whom he had sent emissaries of peace. The identification of these five Greek kings, who were the contemporaries of Devānāmpriya Priyadarśī, forms the basis of the second sheet anchor of Indian chronology. The last Maurya king was uprooted by Puṣyamitra Śuṅga, who established the Śuṅga dynasty. The stupa of Sanchi was enlarged and a terrace was built around it during the rule of the Śuṅgas. Vasudeva Kaṇva uprooted the last Śuṅga king and established the Kaṇva dynasty. The chronology of Maurya, Śuṅga and Kaṇva kings is shown in Table 2.2.

Table: 2.2: Maurya, Śuṅga and Kaṇva kings [8]

King	Period of Reign
Chandragupta Maurya	324-300 BCE
Bindusāra Maurya	300-273 BCE
Aśoka Maurya	273-236 BCE
Other Maurya kings	236-187 BCE
Puṣyamitra Śuṅga	187-151 BCE
Other Śuṅga kings	151-75 BCE
Vasudeva Kaṇva	75-66 BCE
Bhūmimitra Kaṇva	66-52 BCE
Nārāyaṇa Kaṇva	52-40 BCE
Suśarman Kaṇva	40-30 BCE

The Greeks continued their presence at the border during this time, but declared independence from Seleucid kings. The Graeco-Bactrian king Demetrius marched deep inside India during the rule of Puṣyamitra Śuṅga. Another challenge to Puṣyamitra Śuṅga came from the Kaliṅga king Khāravela in Eastern India, who attacked both North and South India during his reign. After the death of Khāravela in 172 BCE, the Śuṅga Empire enjoyed a respite from attacks from Indian kings, but problems on the western border continued and through this border invaders kept pouring in.

2.5 Barbarians at the Gates

During the first century BCE, Bactrian Greek and Indo-Greek rulers were attacked by Parthians (Pahlavas) and Scythians (Śakas). Parthians were attacked by Śakas, who in turn were being attacked by a nomadic group called Yueh-chi. Parthians managed to tame the Śakas, who moved east into India. Śakas were able to establish two branches in India, Northern Śakas controlling areas of Taxila and Mathura, and Western Śakas controlling areas of Malwa and Kathiawar. The chronology of Northern Śakas is presented below in Table 2.3. There is no consensus among historians for the dates of these rulers, so I have presented three different timelines. Modern Chronology I places the beginning of the rule of Azes I in 57 BCE and makes him the founder of an era that later became known as Vikram Samvat. Rājuvula ruled under Azes I as his *satrap* (Kṣatrapa), and later became a great *satrap* (Mahākṣatrapa).

Table 2.3: Northern Śakas

Name	**Modern Chronology I [9]**	**Modern Chronology II [10]**	**Modern Chronology III [11]**
Maues (Moa, Moga)	c. 75-57 BCE	c. 50 BCE	c. 20 BCE to CE 22
Azes I (Aya)	c. 57-35 BCE	c. 38 BCE	c. 5 BCE to CE 30
Azilises (Ayilisha)	c. 50 BCE	c. 10 BCE	c. CE 28-40
Azes II (Aya, Aja)	c. 20-1 BCE	c. CE 5	c. CE 35-79

Western Śakas consisted of two different branches: Kṣaharāta and Kārdamaka Śakas. The first Kṣaharāta ruler was Bhūmaka, who was succeeded by Nahapāna. Nahapāna ruled between 119-125 CE [12] and was defeated by Gautamīputra Sātakarṇi. The Kārdamaka branch of the Western Śakas was established by Chaṣṭana. The chronology of Western Śakas is presented below in Table 2.4 [13]. The rule of Western Śakas lasted till the beginning of the fourth century CE. It is possible that the Western Śakas were overthrown by Sasanians, but this is not certain [14]. Contemporary with

Western Śakas, another foreign power, Kuṣāṇas had established their rule in much of North India starting from Central Asia.

Table 2.4: Kārdamaka Śaka chronology [13]

Kings	Years known	Modern Chronology
Chaṣṭana	52	130 CE
Jayadāman		
Rudradāman	72	150 CE
Dāmajadaśrī		
Jīvadāman	100-120	178-198 CE
Rudrasiṃha I	102-118	180-196 CE
Satyadāman		
Rudrasena I	121-144	199-222 CE
Saṅghadāman	144-145	222-223 CE
Dāmasena	145-158	223-236 CE
Pṛthīvisena	144	222 CE
Dāmajadaśrī II	154-155	232-233 CE
Vīradāman	156-160	234-238 CE
Yaśodāman	160-161	238-239 CE
Vijayasena	161-172	239-250 CE
Dāmajadaśrī III	173-177	251-255 CE
Rudrasena II	177-198	255-276 CE
Viśvasiṃha	197-200	275-278 CE
Bhartṛdāman	200-217	278-295 CE
Viśvasena	215-226	293-304 CE

2.6 The Age of Kuṣāṇas

Around 130 BCE, a wave of the Yueh-Chi tribe was pushed west towards Bactria by a rival tribe, Hiung-nu. The Yueh-Chi settled in Bactria after subduing the Śakas. The Yueh-Chi tribe consisted of five groups, out of which the Kuei-shuang or Kuṣāṇas subdued the rest of the groups. Kuṣāṇas took control of Afghanistan and

Eastern Iran under the leadership of Kujula Kadphises and moved towards India under Wima Kadphises. The Kuṣāṇa Empire reached its zenith under the rule of Kaniṣka. Kuṣāṇa chronology is shown in Table 2.5, which shows two versions of modern chronology. The older version labeled Modern Chronology I considered Kaniṣka to have founded the Śaka era. Recent scholarship has given up on this idea and the revised chronology is shown under Modern Chronology II.

Table 2.5: Kuṣāṇa chronology [15]

	Modern Chronology I	**Modern Chronology II**
	Kaniṣka era starting in 78 CE	Kaniṣka era starting in 127 CE
Kujula Kadphises	c.20 BCE – 20 CE	c.20 – 60 CE
Wima Takto	c.20 – 55 CE	c.60 – 95 CE
Wima Kadphises	c. 55 – 77 CE	c.95 – 126 CE
Kaniṣka I	77/78 – c. 102 CE	126/127 – 152 CE
Huviṣka	c. 102 – 142 CE	c.152 – 191 CE
Vasudeva I	c. 142 – 180 CE	c. 191 – 230 CE
Kaniṣka II	c. 180 – 195 CE	c.230 – 245 CE
Vasiṣka	c. 195 – 210 CE	c.245 – 260 CE
Kaniṣka III	c. 210 – 227 CE	c.260 – 290 CE
Vasudeva II	c. 227 – 260 CE	c. 290 – 320 CE
Shaka	c. 260 – 295 CE	c. 320 – 355 CE
Kipunadha	c. 295 – 320 CE	c. 355 – 375 CE

2.7 The Age of the Sātavāhanas

As the Magadha Empire weakened under the later Śuṅga and Kaṇva rulers, a new power called Sātavāhanas emerged in South India. Sātavāhanas are also known as Āndhras, but they have not identified themselves as Āndhras in any of their inscriptions. The most celebrated Sātavāhana king was Gautamīputra Sātakarṇi, who uprooted the Kṣaharāta Śakas. The Sātavāhana chronology is shown in Table 2.6. There is no unanimity regarding when the rule of the Sātavāhanas started. Two versions of the Sātavāhana chronology are presented to show the differences.

Table 2.6: Sātavāhana chronology

Kings	Modern Chronology I	Modern Chronology II [18]
Simuka (Chimuka)	c. 235-212 BCE [16]	c. 52 - c. 30 BCE
Kṛṣṇa (Kanha)	c. 212-195 BCE [16]	c. 29 - c. 12 BCE
Śātakarṇi I	c. 195-193 BCE [16]	c. 12 BCE - c. 44 CE
Vediśrī and Satiśrī	c. 193-166 BCE [16]	
Śātakarṇi II	166-111 BCE [16]	
Hāla	20-24 CE [16]	
Gautamīputra Śātakarṇi	106-130 CE [17]	c. 61-90 CE
Vāsiṣṭhīputra Pulumāvi	130-159 CE [17]	c. 91-118 CE
Vāsiṣṭhīputra Śātakarṇi		c. 119-147 CE
Vāsiṣṭhīputra Śivaśrī Pulumāvi	159-166 CE [17]	c. 148-155 CE
Vāsiṣṭhīputra Skanda Śātakarṇi	167-174 CE [17]	c. 156-170 CE
Gautamīputra Yajñaśrī Śātakarṇi	174-203 CE [17]	c. 171-199 CE
Gautamīputra Vijaya Śātakarṇi	203-209 CE [17]	c. 200-205 CE
Vāsiṣṭhīputra Chanḍaśrī Śātakarṇi	209-219 CE [17]	c. 206-215 CE
Vāsiṣṭhīputra Vijaya Śātakarṇi		c. 216-225 CE
Vāsiṣṭhīputra Pulumāvi (Pulomā)	219-227 CE [17]	c. 226-232 CE

2.8 The Mighty Guptas

After the fall of the Kuṣāṇas, most of North India was brought under a single rule by the imperial Guptas. The fortunes of the Gupta family rose after the marriage of Chandragupta I with a Lichchhavi princess. The Gupta kingdom expanded further under the rule of Samudragupta and his son Chandragupta II, who married the Nāga princess Kuberanāgā. The daughter of Chandragupta II with Kuberanāgā was Prabhāvatīguptā, who was married to the Vākāṭaka king Rudrasena II. After the death of Rudrasena II, Prabhāvatīguptā ruled as a regent for her minor sons over the Vākāṭaka kingdom. The rule of the Guptas is considered the "Golden Age" of India. The chronology of the Guptas and Vākāṭakas is shown in Tables 2.7 and 2.8 respectively.

Table 2.7: Chronology of Imperial Gupta Kings [19]

Gupta Monarch	**Regnal years**	**Date**
Chandragupta I	1-31	319-50 CE
Samudragupta	31-57	350-76 CE
Chandragupta II	57-96	376-415 CE
Kumāragupta I	96-128	415-447 CE
Ghatotkachagupta	129-136*	448-455 CE
Skandagupta	137-148	456-467 CE
Narasiṃhagupta	148-155	467-474 CE
Kumāragupta II	155-157	474-476 CE
Budhagupta	158-169	477-488 CE
Vainyagupta II	189	506 CE
Viṣnugupta	196	515 CE

*Most historians include this period under Kumāragupta I and consider Skandagupta to have directly succeeded Kumāragupta I.

2.9 Attack of the Hūṇas

In the second half of the fifth century CE the Hephthalites or White Huns called Hūṇas by Indians started their attacks on India. They were repulsed by the Gupta emperor Skandagupta in 460 CE, but returned around 500 CE under the leadership of Toramāṇa. His son Mihirakula succeeded him in 510 CE and continued to expand Hūṇa territory deep inside India.

Table 2.8: Chronology of Vākāṭaka kings [20]

Vākāṭaka King	**Date**
Vindhyaśakti I	250 CE
Pravarasena I	270 CE
Main branch	
Rudrasena I	330 CE
Prithvīsena I	350 CE
Rudrasena II	400 CE
Divākarasena	405 CE
Pravarasena III	420 CE
Narendrasena	450 CE
Prithvīsena II	470 CE
Vatsagulma branch	
Sarvasena	330 CE
Vindhyaśakti II	355 CE
Pravarasena II	400 CE
Son (unnamed)	410 CE
Devasena	450 CE
Harisena	475 CE
Son (unnamed)	500 CE

Mihirakula was defeated in 528 CE by a confederacy of the Gupta emperor Narasiṃhagupta Bālāditya and Malwa ruler Yaśodharmā. Mihirakula died in 542 CE and by the 570s, Hūṇas ceased to be a major threat to Indian polity.

2.10 North India after the Imperial Guptas

The Imperial Gupta Empire disintegrated in the second half of sixth century CE. Maukharies and Later Guptas, who were not related to the Imperial Guptas, fought for supremacy over North India. The chronology of Maukhari rulers is shown in Table 2.9. Īśānavarman was the first Maukhari ruler to assume the imperial title of Mahārājādhirāja. The last Maukhari ruler Grahavarman was married to Rājyaśrī, sister of Harṣavardhana. After the murder of Grahavarman by the Mālava king, Harṣavardhana took over the kingdom of Kannauj and established a North Indian empire. Harṣavardhana ruled from 606 to 647 CE. Later Gupta rulers declared independency after the death of Harṣavardhana and ruled for nearly a century. King Yaśovarman, not related to Maukharies, ruled from Kannauj between 700-740 CE. The next few centuries were dominated by the struggle for supremacy between three powerful kingdoms.

Table 2.9: Maukhari chronology

Kings	Modern Chronology
Harivarman	c. 510-550 CE [21]
Ādityavarman	
Īśvaravarman	
Īśānavarman	c. 550-576 CE [22]
Śarvavarman	c. 576-580 CE [22]
Avantivarman	c. 580-600 CE [22]
Grahavarman	c. 600-605 CE [21]

2.11 The Tripartite Struggle

Between 750 and 1000 CE, Gurjara-Pratihāra kings from West-central India, Rāṣṭrakūṭa kings from South India and Pāla kings from East India fought for control of Kannauj, the seat of power under Harṣavardhana. As the Gurjara-Pratihāra grew in power, they transferred their capital to Kannauj from Bhilmal in Rajasthan. Meanwhile Pāla kings grew in stature starting from Bengal in the second half of the eighth century CE. Pāla kings were strong supporters of Buddhism. They had excellent diplomatic relations with the kings of Shailendra dynasty ruling over the Malay peninsula and the Indonesian archipelago. After taking control of Bihar they moved to take over the imperial throne of Kannauj. The situation became more complicated with the advance of Rāṣṭrakūṭa kings from South India intending to take over Kannauj. This was the first time in Indian history that a South Indian dynasty had tried to dominate the affairs of North India.

The Rāṣṭrakūṭa kings had their capital at Manyakheta, present day Malkhed in Maharashtra. They took the title of "Vallabha", meaning "beloved" and were called Al-Ballahara by Arab historians. An Indian astronomer named Kanaka visited the court of Caliph al-Mansur (754-775 CE) and impressed him so much with his knowledge that two scholars, Ibrahim al-Fazari and Yaqub ibn Tariq were ordered to translate two books by the Indian astronomer Brahmagupta. The Arabic translations of these two astronomy books -- Brahmasphuṭasiddhānta and Khanḍakhādyaka -- were known as Sindhind and Arkand respectively. This was followed by translations of astronomical tables, the number system, and medical treatises such as the Suśruta Saṃhitā in Arabic. A master philosopher of this time was Śankara (788-822 CE), who was the greatest exponent of non-dualistic Vedanta philosophy. The chronologies of Pratihāra, Rāṣṭrakūṭa and Pāla rulers are shown in Tables 2.10 to 2.12.

Table 2.10: Pratihāra chronology

Kings	**Modern Chronology**
Nāgabhaṭa I	730-756 CE [23]
Vatsarāja	780-805 CE [24]
Nāgabhaṭa II	805-833 CE [24]
Rambhadra	833-836 CE [23]
Mihirabhoja I	836-885 CE [23]
Mahendrapāla I	885-910 CE [24]
Mihirabhoja II	910-912 CE [24]
Mahīpāla I	912-944 CE [24]
Mahendrapāla II	945-948 CE [24]
Devapāla	948-949 CE [24]
Vināyakapāla II	953-954 CE [24]
Mahīpāla II	955 CE [23]
Vijayapāla	960 CE [23]

Table 2.11: Rāṣṭrakūṭa chronology [25]

Kings	**Modern Chronology**
Dantidurga	754 CE
Kṛṣṇa I	760 -773 CE
Govinda II	773-780 CE
Dhruva	780-793 CE
Govinda III	793-814 CE
Amoghavarṣa I	814-878 CE
Kṛṣṇa II	878-914 CE
Indra III	914-927 CE
Govinda IV	927-936 CE
Amoghavarṣa III	936-939 CE
Kṛṣṇa III	939-967 CE
Khoṭṭiga	967-972 CE
Karkka II	972-991 CE

Table 2.12: Pāla chronology [26]

Kings	**Modern Chronology**
Gopāla	750-775 CE
Dharmapāla	775-810 CE
Devapāla	810-847 CE
Śūrapāla I	847-860 CE
Vigrahapāla	860-861 CE
Nārayaṇapāla	861-917 CE
Rājyapāla	917-952 CE
Gopāla II	952-972 CE
Vigrahapāla II	972-977 CE
Mahīpāla I	977-1027 CE
Nayapāla	1027-43 CE
Vigrahapāla III	1043-70 CE
Mahīpāla II	1070-71 CE
Śūrapāla II	1071-72 CE
Rāmapāla	1072-1126 CE
Kumārapāla	1126-28 CE
Gopāla III	1128-43 CE
Madanapāla	1143-61 CE
Govindapāla	1161-65 CE
Palapāla	1165-1200 CE

2.12 The Paramāra Dynasty

As the Pratihāra and Rāṣṭrakūṭa dynasties declined, other kingdoms rose to take their place. The most prominent among them were the kings of the Paramāra dynasty. They ruled from Dhārā Nagarī, present day Dhar in Madhya Pradesh. The most famous king of this dynasty was Bhoja Paramāra, who has written treatises on a number of subjects. The chronology of Paramāra kings is shown in Table 2.13.

Table 2.13: Paramāra chronology [27]

Kings	**Modern Chronology**
Vākpatirāja I*	c. 895-920 CE
Vairīsiṃha	c. 920-945 CE
Sīyaka	c. 945-973 CE
Vākpati-Munja**	c. 973-995 CE
Sindhurāja	c. 995-1000 CE
Bhojadeva	c. 1000-1055 CE
Jayasiṃha	c. 1055-1070 CE
Udayāditya	c. 1070-1093 CE
Naravarman	c. 1093-1134 CE
Yasovarman	c.1134-1142 CE
Jayavarman	c. 1142-1143 CE
Lakṣmīvarman	c. 1143-1155 CE
Hariśchandra	c. 1155-1186 CE
Udayavarman	c. 1186-1215 CE
Vindhyavarman	c.1187-1194 CE
Subhatavarman	c. 1194-1209 CE
Arjunavarman	c. 1210-1215 CE
Devapāla	c. 1218-1235 CE
Jaitugi	c. 1235-1255 CE
Jayasiṃha- Jayavarman II	c. 1255-1275 CE
Arjunavarman	c. 1275 CE

* also called Kṛṣṇarāja

** also called Utpala

I will end the chronological summary of official Indian history here, as the modern chronological history of India is on firmer ground after the Islamic rule in India. The examination of evidence that backs up the official chronology of Indian history forms the subject matter of the next chapter.

Notes:

1. Jones (1793).
2. Majumdar et al. (1996).
3. Majumdar et al. (2001).
4. Majumdar et al. (1997).
5. Majumdar et al. (1993).
6. Avari (2007).
7. Majumdar et al. (2001): 36-38.
8. Majumdar et al. (2001): 54-100.
9. Pal (1986): 85-88.
10. Marshall (2013): 25.
11. Majumdar et al. (2001): 127.
12. Majumdar et al. (2001): 180.
13. Majumdar et al. (2001): 178-190.
14. Majumdar et al. (2001): 190.
15. Loeschner (2008).
16. Middleton (2015): 828.
17. Majumdar et al. (2001): 191-216.
18. Shastri (1999): 35.
19. Willis (2005).
20. Mirashi (1963): vi.
21. Srivastava (2007): 452-453.
22. Majumdar et al. (1997): 70.
23. Majumdar et al. (1993): 19-43.
24. Srivastava (2007): 505-507, 563-564.
25. Majumdar et al. (1993): 1-18.
26. Bagchi (1993): 50-51.
27. Trivedi (1991): 9-53.

"You have got to know the rules to break them. That's what I'm here for, to demolish the rules but to keep the tradition."

- Alexander McQueen

3. THE PRIVILEGE OF ABSURDITY

To repeat, modern Indian chronology rests on two pillars, first being the identification of Sandrokottos with Chandragupta Maurya, the founder of Maurya dynasty, making him a contemporary of Alexander the Great, and second being the identification of Devānāmpriya Priyadarśī with Aśoka Maurya, making him a contemporary of Antiochus II. Regarding the first pillar, historians know very well that Sandrokottos could be identified with either Chandragupta Maurya of Maurya Dynasty or Chandragupta I of the Imperial Gupta Dynasty. Thus, we have to deal with the second pillar on which all of Indian chronology rests. In over 175 years since the identification of Devānāmpriya Priyadarśī with Aśoka Maurya, a satisfactory alternative has not been found. If a credible alternative is found, and the second pillar of Indian chronology develops fissures, the edifice of Indian chronology will crumble like a house of cards. Then we can begin to develop the framework of an alternative chronology, which will be acceptable to modern historians. The development of this alternative framework is the objective of this book. First, let me begin by pointing out what is wrong with the current framework of Indian history.

Currently, Chandragupta Maurya, the founder of Maurya Dynasty, is placed towards the last quarter of fourth century BCE, while Chandragupta I, the founder of the Imperial Gupta Dynasty is placed in the first half of fourth century CE. The two Chandraguptas are separated in time by roughly 650 years. Let's suppose that modern historians have made an error in developing Indian chronology based on the identification of Sandrokottos with Chandragupta Maurya instead of Chandragupta I.

What would be the possible implications of such an error? I have not come across a careful and rigorous discussion of such an error in my research on this topic spanning over ten years. In fact, the first thing that came to my mind, after I had discovered that Devānāmpriya Priyadarśī was not Aśoka Maurya, but some other king, who has never been identified as Devānāmpriya Priyadarśī was this possibility. If we are going to move historical figures forward by more than six centuries, we are going to create a vacuum somewhere: because if there were people identified who are not there anymore, what will be the consequence?

Does such a vacuum exist in Indian history? I believe it does, and it is the period before the sixth century BCE. Indian history actually starts in sixth century BCE with Buddha and the kings who were his contemporaries. The chronology before the Buddha is rather vague and amorphous. We find no names of any historical persons before the sixth century BCE. There is only literary history before this period without any names attached to any event. The names that we find adduced to the sixth century BCE may as well fit the context in the twelfth century BCE.

Next, if Indian historians have moved people forward by six centuries, it would result in a crowding of kings elsewhere, putting some people where other people are already in place. It should not come as a surprise that this crowding happens/can be observed in the sixth century CE! Here we find four mighty empires of Imperial Guptas, Aulikaras, Maukharies and Later Guptas vying for the same space in time. While the Imperial Guptas and Aulikaras were contemporaries, as were Maukharies and Later Guptas, there is no evidence that the first two were the contemporaries of the latter two. The displacement of people in time would create false contemporaries. Once we shift people from where they belong to where they don't, we are going to create contemporaries out of people who have no way of knowing each other. So, how does Indian history deal with such situations? Historians have made assumptions or posited evidence where none exists. Here are some examples related to the Imperial Guptas, Aulikaras, Maukharies and Later Guptas:

"Since the Aphsad inscription does not contain any reference to a Gupta monarch while describing Mahasenagupta's military campaigns in the seat, it seems to be ***quite likely that*** *all the vestiges of the Imperial Guptas were wiped out by the time of Mahasenagupta's campaigns, and that some of the Gupta possessions in North Bengal were, in all probability, wrested by Susthitavarman or one of his predecessors." [1]*

"A set of three Maukhari feudatories, ***perhaps of the Guptas****, are mentioned in the Barabar and Nagarjuni hill inscriptions, which are inscribed in the characters of the fifth century AD." [2]*

"... it does not seem unreasonable to hold that about the close of the fifth century AD the Maukharis were still settled in Magadha round the Gaya region, and that they were feudatories to ***some power – very possibly*** *the Later Guptas – as even at this time they were powerful enough to curb the rise of an independent state in the very heart of their home countries." [3]*

"It should be remembered that the time of both Iśānavarmā and Jivitagupta I falls between 520 to 540 AD. This is exactly the time of Malwa's Aulikara emperor Yaśodharmā (known date 532 AD) and he has been given credit for winning the region from Himalayas in the north to Brahmaputra river to the east. Clearly he would have won Bengal as well. It is clear from this fact that Jivitagupta I,

Crown prince Iśānavarmā and Malwa's Yaśodharmā, ***all three claim to have won*** *Himalayan region and Bengal between 520 to 540 A.D." [4]*

From the above, imagine how could it be possible for three dynasties to claim the same area at the same time? The following quote about Dhruvasena I of Maitraka Dynasty of Vallabhī is a classic example of the cluelessness of modern historians regarding who ruled when and who was whose contemporary.

"The inscriptions of Dhruvasena I dated Gupta era 206 to 226 (525 to 545 A.D.) mention him under the service of a supreme Lord (Paramabhattāraka Pādānudhyāta). This supreme lord has been identified as Yashodharmā by Fleet [Indian Antiquary, Vol. 15, p. 187, Bombay], Budhagupta by Cunningham [Journal of the Asiatic Society of Bengal, Vol. 58, p. 97], Hūṇas by Smith [Early History of India, p. 314], Harisena Vākāṭaka by Virajī [Early History of Saurashtra, pp. 27-29], Vainyagupta by Budhaprakasha [Annals of the Bhandarakara Oriental Research Institute, Vol. 18, p. 133, Puna] and Narasiṃhagupta Bālāditya by Sinha [Decline of the Kingdom of Magadha, 1954, Patna, p. 90]" [5]

This brings us to another consequence of the false chronology, and that is when different people claim sovereignty over the same region at the same time, as above. It is the same problem in the context of the Śaka rulers and Kuṣāṇas, who have been made contemporaneous by modern historians, as can be seen below:

"Rasesh Jamindar has advanced a theory that Kanishka existed after Rudradaman perhaps in the second half of the 2nd century. He argues that Rudradaman's domination over Sindhu, Sui Vihar (including Multan) and Kanishka's rule over Multan and Sui Vihar is not possible at the same time. Secondly Rudradaman could not have defeated Yaudheyas after crossing the Kushana territory who were occupying the Punjab area."[6]

Even though modern historians make the Śaka Kṣatrapas and Mahākṣatrapas the sub-ordinates of Kuṣāṇa rulers, the fact is that Kuṣāṇas have not mentioned Śakas, and the Śakas do not know of any Kuṣāṇas. A similar case is found of some small rulers minting their own coins right under the nose of the mighty Imperial Guptas:

> *"The rule of Shakas and Shiladas came to an end in c. 340 A.D. with the rise of a tribe, which is sometimes described as the Little Kushana and sometimes as Kidara Kushana. ... Numismatic evidence shows that a number of petty rulers like Kritavirya, Shiladitya, Sarvayashas, Bhasvan, Kushala and Prakasha were ruling in the Punjab during the first half of the 5th century A.D. They were probably Kidara Kushana rulers, for the name Kidara appears on their coins on the obverse." [7]*

If these minor rulers were subject to the edicts of the Imperial Guptas it is doubtful, if not impossible that the Imperial Guptas would let feudatories mint their own coins. We can conclude therefore that this was not the time of the Imperial Guptas. In the 5th century CE, the rule of Kuṣāṇas had ended, the Kuṣāṇa Empire had disintegrated, and North India was under the sway of petty rulers. Another instance of independent rulers in the dominion of the Imperial Guptas at the zenith of their power is the following:

> *"Unlike the Maharajas of Valkha, Subandhu does not refer to any suzerain even in a general manner, which shows that he was an independent ruler. In 416-417 AC, the Gupta power had, no doubt, reached its peak. Chandragupta II was dead at the time and was succeeded by his son Kumaragupta I, but there is no reason to suppose that the Gupta dominion had suffered any diminution at the beginning of the latter's reign. It may, therefore, be asked how Kumaragupta allowed Subandhu to enjoy independence just on the border of the Avanti province which was undoubtedly under Gupta rule at the time." [8]*

The answer to the above conundrum is simple. They were not contemporaries, but have been made so by the false chronology. It is true that we don't have a reliable written history of India from ancient sources, but we do have lots of information about Indian history from literary sources, inscriptions, numismatics and archaeology. Let's consider all this information, which comes in bits and pieces, as parts of a gigantic puzzle. If we have the framework of history right, all these pieces will fit together and fall in their proper places. On the other hand, if we don't have the framework of history right, we will be force-fitting these puzzle pieces. Indian history is full of examples of this force-fitting. Let me list some of them in chronological fashion.

3.1 Aryan Invasion Theory

In traditional Indian history there is no record of ancient Indians arriving from outside the region. Vedic people lived in Sapta Sindhu or the land of the seven rivers. Indus and Saraswatī were the most prominent among these rivers. The sites of Indus Valley Civilization (IVC) are also on the banks of these two rivers. Naturally, IVC was Vedic civilization. However, modern historians claimed that Vedic people were invaders, who destroyed IVC inhabited by Dravidian people. After two hundred years of searching, historians have found no proof of any such invasion/s and quietly replaced the term "invasion" with "migration". The contention, however, is still the same: that the Vedic people came from outside the Indus/Saraswatī region.

Based on the linguistic similarity of Sanskrit and ancient European languages such as Greek and Latin, a number of languages have been included in the Indo-European family. Taking this concept further into the past, it is proposed that a group of people called Proto-Indo-Europeans spoke a language called Proto-Indo-European (PIE) language, the progenitor of the Indo-European languages. On the other hand, traditional Indian history claims that

India was the cradle of civilization and Sanskrit is the mother of all Indian languages. It may turn out that PIE is a hypothetical language that was spoken by an imagined people, and nothing more. India has always been highly populated, and we can posit that India must have been the original homeland of the Aryans, not some cold, deserted place in Central Asia, which was never densely populated to begin with. Herodotus, the father of history, says this about Indians in Book III.89-96 [9]:

> *"Of the Indians, the population is by far the greatest of all nations whom we know of, and they paid a tribute proportionately larger than all the rest, 360 talents of gold dust; this was the twentieth division."*

There was no Aryan invasion of India, many now argue, but rather Vedic people went out of the Indian homeland (Out of India/OIT), which resulted in the proliferation of Indo-European languages. If the chronology presented in my books is accepted by historians after verification, it will offer us an opportunity to trace the movement of Aryans out of India, starting in about 1900 BCE.

3.2 Vedāṅga Jyotiṣa

Vedāṅga Jyotiṣa, composed by Lāgadha, is the earliest Indian text on astronomy. It makes an observation as follows [10]:

> *"The Sun and the Moon turn towards the north at the first point of the Dhaniṣṭhā Nakṣatra, and towards the south at the middle point of Āśleṣā, and this always happens in the months of Māgha and Śrāvaṇa."*

Various dates are given for this observation, between 1370 BCE to 1150 BCE [11]. All of these dates are problematic for accepted chronology, as the Vedas are supposed to have been compiled around 1000 BCE or later, and the Vedāṅga Jyotiṣa is posterior to the Vedas. Historians have tried to wiggle out of this situation by claiming that the text was written much later and presumably the observation is from memory. I will show in the next chapter that this observation was made much earlier than the currently accepted dates. This creates an insurmountable problem for the official chronology.

3.3 Buddha

According to the Hindu Purāṇas, Gautama Buddha lived during the 19th century BCE as described below [12]:

> *"Buddha's birth date was 1887 B.C. and Buddha's renunciation in 1858 B.C. In the reign of the 32nd king, Bimbisara between 1852 and 1814 B.C., Buddha became the "The Enlightened" and began to preach his new faith. During the reign of the 33rd king, Ajata Satru, from 1814 to 1787 B.C., in that interval, Buddha's Nirvana happened in 1807 B.C."*

We have seen in the first chapter that Sir William Jones considered the date of birth of Buddha to be 1027 BCE. The chronology was revised subsequent to his identification of the Indian king Sandrokottos from Greek accounts with Chandragupta Maurya in 1793. We have the following testimony from Fa-Hien, who visited India between 399-414 CE [13]:

> *"The monks asked Fa-Hien if it could be known when the Law of Buddha first went to the east. He replied, 'When I asked the people of those countries about it, they all said that it had been handed down by their fathers from of old that, after the setting up of the image of Maitreya Bodhisattva, there were Shramans of India who crossed this river, carrying with them Sutras and books of Discipline. Now the image was set up rather more than three hundred years after the nirvana of Budha, which may be referred to the reign of king Ping of the chow dynasty."*

James Legge clarifies this paragraph in the footnote as follows [14]:

> *"As king Ping's reign lasted from B.C. 750 to 719, this would place the death of Buddha in the eleventh century B.C., whereas recent inquiries place it between B.C. 480 and 470, a year or two, or a few years, after that of Confucius, so that the two great Masters of the East were really contemporaries."*

Thus the Chinese tradition favors the date of birth of the Buddha in 11th century BCE. Modern historians place the birth of Buddha in 6th century BCE sometime between 567-563 BCE and his death in 5th century BCE sometime between 487-483 BCE. According to Buddhist traditions, he lived for 80 years. Since Indian and Chinese dates are too early, modern historians have come up with this strange idea that Ceylonese/Sri Lankan dates are more reliable. It goes against common sense that the place farthest from the birth place of Buddha will preserve the most authentic date of his birth. The fact is that the Ceylonese texts "Dīpavaṃśa" and "Mahāvaṃśa" were written in the 4th century and 5th to 6th century respectively, which are of very late origin. These texts in turn are based on texts that are no longer available. There is simply no reason for Ceylonese texts to be more reliable than Indian, Chinese, and Nepalese texts.

Modern historians have calculated the date of the Buddha from the date of Aśoka Maurya. Since the date of coronation of Aśoka has been fixed as ~268 BCE, they searched for texts for the date of the Buddha that would be consistent with the date of Aśoka's coronation. They found in Ceylonese texts that coronation of Piyadassi took place 218 years after the death of the Buddha. Working backwards, historians calculated the date of death of Buddha in ~486 BCE and his birth 80 years earlier in ~566 BCE. However, the same Ceylonese texts that mention the 218 years between the death of Buddha and coronation of Piyadassi also say that the Buddha died in 544/543 BCE. If we take that date as reliable, then coronation of Aśoka Maurya took place 218 years later in 326/325 BCE, which is around the time of the invasion of

India by Alexander and much earlier than the time of the five Greek kings mentioned in the rock edicts of Piyadassi.

There is another piece of evidence that shows that the time of the Buddha was several centuries earlier than where modern historians have placed him. This evidence relates to the expulsion of Buddhists by the followers of Zarathustra. Here is what Al-Biruni has said [15]:

> *"In former times, Khurasan, Persis, Irak, Mosul, the country up to the frontier of Syria, was Buddhistic, but then Zarathustra went forth from Adharbaijan and preached Magism in Balkh (Baktra). His doctrine came into favour with king Gushtasp, and his son Isfendiyad spread the new faith both in the east and west, both by force and by treaties. He founded fire temples through his whole empire, from the frontiers of China to those of the Greek empire. The succeeding kings made their religion (i.e. Zoroastrianism) the obligatory state religion for Persis and Irak. In consequence, the Buddhists were banished from these countries, and had to emigrate to the countries east of Balkh."*

The date of Zarathustra is itself uncertain, but it is no later than 6th century BCE. Since Buddhism had to spread in the regions listed above starting from a faraway place in eastern India, Buddhism can be said to have originated many centuries before the date of Zarathustra.

3.4 Pāṇini

The date of Pāṇini, one of the greatest intellectuals in human history and renowned for his work on Sanskrit grammar called Aṣtādhyāyī, is also subject to controversy. Such was the impact of his work that the form and structure of Sanskrit language was fixed for millennia to come. Modern scholarship places him somewhere in the three centuries between the 7th and the 4th century BCE as presented below:

> *"Panini is the best known of the Indian linguists. His date is uncertain, but around 600 BC or later has been suggested in the light of the evidence available. His Sanskrit grammar has been described as 'one of the greatest monuments of human intelligence'."* [16]

> *"Hwen Thsang next visited So-lo-tu-lo, or Salatura, the birthplace of the celebrated grammarian Panini, which he says was 20 li, or 3 (and) 1/3 miles, to the north-west of Ohind. In January 1848, during a day's halt at the village of Lahor, which is exactly four miles to the north-east of Ohind, I procured several Greek and Indo-Scythian coins, from which it may be inferred, with some certainty, that the place is at least as old as the time of Panini himself, or about B.C. 350."* [17]

Pāṇini was a native of Salatura, a village in Gāndhāra. There are inscriptions from Persian emperors Darius I (522-486 BCE) and Xerxes (486-465 BCE) that Gāndhāra was part of the Persian Empire during their times. According to Herodotus, considered the "Father of History" and a contemporary of Artaxerxes (465-424 BCE), the successor of Xerxes, Gāndhāra continued to be part of the Persian Empire during the reign of Artaxerxes. Gāndhāra continued to be under Persian rule all the way up to Alexander's invasion of Persia [18]. However, on one hand, Pāṇini mentions Gāndhāra, the place of his birth, as an independent kingdom [19], and on the other hand, Āryamañjuśrīmūlakalpa, a medieval text, declares Pāṇini to be the contemporary of Nanda rulers [20]. So if Pāṇini was the contemporary of Nanda rulers and his place of birth was independent at his time, then Nanda rulers must have been ruling before Gāndhāra was annexed by Persian rulers in the 6th century BCE.

3.5 Ādi Śankarāchārya

Ādi Śankarāchārya was one of the greatest intellectuals India has produced. He was the greatest proponent of Advaita Vedānta philosophy. He engaged the scholars of various schools of philosophy such as Mimānsā, Sāṅkhya and Buddhism in debate and established the supremacy of Advaita Vedānta. According to traditional sources, Ādi Śankarāchārya lived between 509-477 BCE. However, according to modern historians, Ādi Śankarāchārya lived between 788-820 CE. This is based on Ādi Śankarāchārya quoting Buddhist logician Dharmakīrtti verbatim, who in turn has been quoted by Chinese traveller Xuan Zang in 7th century CE. The real reason the traditional date is not acceptable to modern historians is that Ādi Śankarāchārya cannot be the contemporary of Buddha. If the time of Buddha was several centuries before the currently accepted date, then the objection to traditional date of Ādi Śankarāchārya can be worked out. If Ādi Śankarāchārya had indeed lived in 9th century CE, he would certainly be aware of Islam, but he is completely silent about it.

3.6 Vikramāditya

According to the Indian tradition, King Vikramāditya had extirpated the Śakas, who had invaded India. He was a very generous king and a paragon of virtues. There were nine gems, people with extraordinary skills in their field, in his court. Two of these gems were Varāhamihira, astronomer par excellence, and Kālidāsa, poet par excellence. Vikrama era, still in use in India, was instituted to commemorate the death of King Vikramāditya in 57 BCE.

Modern history denies the existence of King Vikramāditya in 57 BCE. Varāhamihira has been placed in early sixth century CE and Kālidāsa has been made the court poet of Chandragupta II Vikramāditya, who ruled between 376-415 CE. According to modern history books, Azes, a Śaka ruler, was the founder of the Vikrama era [21].

"Azes (Aya in Kharosthi) was another powerful Śaka ruler in the Northwest who initiated a dynastic era beginning in 58/57 B.C.

> *which later became identified with the so-called Vikrama era still used in South Asia."*

However, according to recent research by Falk and Bennet [22], Azes era didn't start in 57 BCE. This has created a strange situation for modern historians, as they have to come up with a ruler to whom they can attribute the establishment of the Vikrama era.

3.7 Śālivāhana Śaka

According to Indian tradition, Śālivāhana Śaka era was started to commemorate the extirpation of the evil Śakas by Gautamiputra Śātakarṇi. However, modern historians have made the Kuṣāṇa emperor Kaniṣka the founder of the Śālivāhana Śaka era [23].

> *"Opinions differ, but it is probable that the Saka era of A.D. 78 dates from the accession or coronation of Kanishka, the Shaka king. Indian authors use the term Saka vaguely to denote all foreigners from beyond the passes, and would have had no hesitation in calling a Kushana a Saka. In later ages the era was known as that of Salivahana."*

This theory is now being abandoned as a verse from Yavanajātaka written by Sphujidhvaja gives a relationship between the Śaka era and the Kuṣāna era [24]. Harry Falk has proposed the starting date of 127 CE for the Kuṣāṇa era even though, according to Yavanajātaka, it should be 227 CE.

3.8 Nāgārjuna

Nāgārjuna, the famous Buddhist philosopher, is considered to have lived around 150 CE. He is said to have taught at the Nālandā University. Nālandā University was founded by Śakrāditya according to a seal [25]. This is also corroborated by Xuan Zang, the famous Chinese traveller, as follows [26]:

> *"After the nirvana of Buddha an old king of this country called Śakrāditya, from a principle of loving obedience of Buddha, built this convent. After his decease his son Buddhagupta-rāja seized the throne, and continued the vast undertaking; he built towards the south, another Saṅghārāma. Then his son (successor) Tathāgata-rāja built a Saṅghārāma to the eastward. Next, his son (or, direct descendent) Bālāditya built a Saṅghārāma to the north-east. Afterwards the king, seeing some priests who came from the country of China to receive his religious offerings, was filled with gladness, and he gave up his royal estate and became a recluse. His son Vajra succeeded and built another Saṅghārāma to the north. After him a king of Mid-India built by the side of this another Saṅghārāma. Thus six kings in connected succession added to these structures. … The priests dwelling here, are as a body, naturally (or, spontaneously) dignified and grave, so that during the 700 years since the foundation of the establishment, there has been no single case of guilty rebellion against the rules."*

Śakrāditya was another name of Kumāragupta I Mahendrāditya, who lived in the 5th century CE according to modern historians. How did Nāgārjuna teach at the world-renowned Nālandā University in 2nd century CE, if the university was founded three centuries later by Kumāragupta I? As Xuan Zang came to India in the 7th century CE, and Kumāragupta I ruled in the 5th century CE, it would be only two centuries since the establishment of Nālandā University on the arrival of Xuan Zang. So why did he say that the university had already existed for seven centuries? This is clearly against the accepted chronology and fits the alternate chronology in which Chandragupta I of Imperial Gupta dynasty was the contemporary of Alexander the Great and therefore his great grandson Kumāragupta I ruled in the 2nd century BCE.

In this chapter, I have discussed some of the pieces of evidence that do not fit in the scheme of currently accepted history. When

we have discovered the correct chronology of Indian history, all these pieces will fall in their proper places like a jig-saw puzzle.
I will start by putting one of these puzzle pieces in its proper place, as it is the force-fitting of this puzzle piece that started me on this long journey to reconstruct ancient history of India – the correct dates of Varāhamihira, the foremost astronomer of his time.

Notes

1. Ganguli (1987): 123.
2. Tripathi (1942): 289.
3. Tripathi (1964): 31-32.
4. Goyala (1986): 23-24 (translated from Hindi).
5. Goyala (1988): 335-336 (translated from Hindi).
6. Sagar (1992): 171.
7. Majumdar and Altekar (1967): 21-23.
8. Mirashi (1955): xxxix-xl.
9. McCrindle (1901): 1.
10. Yajus Vedāṅga Jyotiṣa, Verse 7.
11. Witzel (2001)
12. Venkatachelam (1956): 17.
13. Legge (1886): 27.
14. Legge (1886): 27, Footnote 5.
15. Sachau (1910): 21.
16. Robins (2013): 427.
17. Cunningham (1871): 57-58.
18. Sethna (2000): 121-172.
19. Aṣṭādhyāyī IV.1.169, IV.1.133 and IV.3.93.
20. Jayaswal (1934): 14.
21. Srinivasan (2007): 71.
22. Falk and Bennett (2009).
23. Smith (1915): 74.
24. Falk (2001).
25. http://en.wikipedia.org/wiki/Nalanda, retrieved on August 2, 2015.
26. Beal (1911): 110-112.

"We should not keep forever on the public road, going only where others have gone; we should leave the beaten track occasionally and enter the woods. Every time you do that you will be certain to find something that you have never seen before. Of course, it will be a little thing; but do not ignore it. Follow it up, explore all round it; one discovery will lead to another, and before you know it you will have something worth thinking about to occupy your mind, for all really big discoveries are the results of thought."

- Alexander Graham Bell

4. FROM PERSIA WITH LOVE

Varāhamihira was one of the greatest astronomers of ancient India. I came across the following verse by Varāhamihira in 2001 [1]:

> *"āsanmaghāsu munayaḥ śāsati pṛthvīn yudhiṣṭhire nṛpatau*
> *ṣaḍdvikapañcadviyutaḥ śakakālastasya rājyasya."*

This is a well-studied verse in Indology as it has the potential to seriously challenge modern Indian chronology. The verse can have two different interpretations, and the chronology of Indian history depends on which interpretation is correct. Let us start by the English translation of this verse provided by Alexander Cunningham in 1883 CE [2]:

> *"The seven seers were in Maghā when king Yudhiṣṭhira ruled the earth, and the period of that king is 2526 years before the Śaka era."*

Alexander Cunningham and all proponents of the modern Indian chronology interpret this verse as defining the time of King Yudhiṣṭhira, eldest brother among the five Pāṇḍavas, who fought the Mahābhārata war against his cousins turned adversaries,

Kauravas. They take the beginning of Śaka era in 78 CE and define the time of Yudhiṣṭhira according to Varāhamihira as 2526 years before 78 CE or 2448 BCE.

The proponents of the alternative chronology argue that the verse is not defining the times of Yudhiṣṭhira, but the Śaka era, as the time of Yudhiṣṭhira was well established in Varāhamihira's mind. As Yudhiṣṭhira participated in the Mahābhārata war and the Kali age followed shortly after the Mahābhārata war, the time of Yudhiṣṭhira will be close to 3102 BCE – the traditionally accepted date of the Mahābhārata war. If we count 2526 years from 3102 BCE, then we get 576 BCE as the date of Śaka era as defined by Varāhamihira. There is need for a correction here as follows. Yudhiṣṭhira is supposed to have lived for 25 years after the start of the Kali age and the era named after him, Yudhiṣṭhira era, starts from the date Yudhiṣṭhira left this world. Thus the Yudhiṣṭhira era starts from 3077 BCE, 25 years after the start of Kali era. If we count from this date for Yudhiṣṭhira, we get 551 BCE as the date of Śaka era as defined by Varāhamihira.

The question is which of these interpretations is right. Our next clue comes from Varāhamihira himself in the preceding verse to the verse quoted above [3], where Varāhamihira says that he is following the views of the senior Garga. So what did the senior Garga say? Let's follow Alexander Cunningham again to find out [4]:

> *"But unluckily for Varaha Mihira his commentator, Bhatta Utpala, has given us the very words of Garga, who simply says:*
>
> > "At the junction of the Kali and Dwapara ages, the virtuous sages, who delight in protecting the people, stood at the asterism, over which the Pitris preside (that is Magha)."
>
> *On comparing this quotation with Varaha's statement, we see at once that he has suppressed Garga's mention of the beginning of the*

> *Kali-Yuga to suit his astronomical fancies. Now Garga states most explicitly that the Seven Rishis were in Magha at the beginning of the Kali-Yuga, and says nothing whatever about Yudhiṣṭhira. But the fact that the Rishis were in Magha at the time of the Great War was too well known to be altered, and so Varaha accepts this, while he quietly ignores Garga's statement about the Kali-Yuga."*

So Varāhamihira is following the senior Garga, who has said that when the Kali age started, the seven sages were in Maghā asterism. Varāhamihira is saying that Yudhiṣṭhira was ruling when the seven sages were in the Maghā asterism. Logically, it follows that according to Varāhamihira, when the seven sages were in Maghā asterism then Yudhiṣṭhira was ruling and the Kali age started. There is no confusion whatsoever about when the Kali age started, according to Hindu beliefs, which is 3102 BCE. Thus it seems more likely that Varāhamihira is defining the Śaka era and not the age of Yudhiṣṭhira, and it is Cunnigham who had not understood him and tried to insult him on top of that.

I fail to understand what astronomical fancies ancient Indian astronomers had that these colonial era scholars keep referring to. Astronomers as well as other scientists worked closely with religious scholars in ancient India, and that is why there was no case of persecution of scientists in India as was the case in Europe. This is also the reason why so many of Hindu beliefs and customs have firm scientific basis that modern Hindus, who derive their knowledge of Hinduism from the West, have failed to appreciate. The Mahābhārata war, involvement of Pāṇḍavas including Yudhiṣṭhira in this war, the involvement of Lord Kṛṣṇa in an advisory capacity to Pāṇḍavas in the war, the start of the Kali age only after the demise of Lord Kṛṣṇa, all of these events are so interwoven in Hindu scriptures including Purāṇas and Mahābhārata that it is inconceivable that Varāhamihira would separate the start of the Kali age and the reign of Yudhiṣṭhira by over six hundred years without offering an explanation.

The Indian tradition is nearly unanimous that Kaliyuga started shortly after the Mahābhārata war. Only one person, Kalhaṇa, deviates from that tradition. Kalhaṇa wrote the book Rājataraṅgiṇī in the 12th century CE detailing the history of Kashmir. He says that 653 years had passed after the beginning of the Kali era, when the Kauravas and Pāṇḍavas lived [5]. He further states that some people think that the Bhārata war took place at the end of Dwāpara age, but this is due to mistake in their calculations [6]. But how does Kalhaṇa know that other people were wrong and he was right? He gives the clue in the next verse, where he says that if the years of reigns of all the kings of the Kali era are added up to his time, then nothing is left [7]. We see that when Kalhaṇa had deviated from accepted tradition, he tells so and gives a reason for that. If Varāhamihira had done so, then he would definitely have given an explanation. Since he didn't, it is logical to conclude that it was Kalhaṇa who misinterpreted Varāhamihira's verse and added confusion because his list of kings of Kashmir was presumably incomplete and fell short by over six hundred years assuming the start of Mahābhārata war 36 years before 3102 BCE. In fact, we have proof by Cunningham himself that it was Kalhaṇa who separated the Kali age from Mahābhārata and Yudhiṣṭhira by over six centuries and not Varāhamihira [8].

> *"The Purāṇas, and the practice of all the people who still use this cycle, excepting only the Kashmiris, agree in making the era of Yudhishthira the same as the Kali-Yuga."*

As Kalhaṇa was from Kashmir, his idea got a foothold in Kashmir, but was not accepted anywhere else. If Varāhamihira had proposed this idea, this reckoning should have found support around Ujjain. This was clearly not so.

Modern historians assert that Varāhamihira used the Śaka era starting in 78 CE. However, according to traditional historians he used the the Śaka era starting in 550 BCE and specifically name

Cyrus the Great as the Śaka king after whom Varāhamihira has named this Śaka era. Here is a relevant quote [9]:

> *"Even Western scholars agreed that either Vikrama Era or Salivahana Era was not prevalent at the time of Garga. So the Śaka Era related in the Sloka is neither Vikrama nor Salivahana Era and this fact is approved by all the historians. That is the age of the Persian Emperor, Cyrus, which began in 550 B.C."*

The difference between these two Śaka eras is 628 years. Varāhamihira has said that he wrote Pañchasiddhāntikā in 427 Śaka [10] and commentator Amaraja has added that he died in 509 Śaka in his commentary on Brahmagupta's Khandakhādyaka.

As the difference between these two dates is 82 years, some scholars think that he was born in 427 Śaka. It is certainly possible that he lived long and may have written Pañchasiddhāntikā in his twenties. In that case he attained adulthood by 505 CE and died in 587 CE according to modern historians using Śaka era starting in 78 CE. Alternatively, he attained adulthood by 123 BCE and died in 41 BCE using a Śaka era starting in 550 BCE. We should note that my calculations show 551 BCE as the start of original Śaka era, but Venkatachelam takes it as 550 BCE as he takes the Yudhiṣṭhira era to start in 3076 BCE. The difference of one year can result either from Christian era starting in January and Hindu eras starting at some other month in the year, for example in October with the festival of lights, or the use of the current year instead of the previous year.

It is at this point in my research that I asked myself the following: Varāhamihira was one of the greatest astronomers of ancient India and has written so many treatises on astronomy and astrology. Since 628 years is a long time for detecting changes in astronomical observations, did Varāhamihira report any astronomical observation that can be used to settle this debate? So, I started reading the books by Varāhamihira keeping an eye for such an observation, and sure enough I found it in the Bṛhat Saṃhitā itself.

4.1 Precession of the Solstices

I was looking for an astronomical observation that would settle the debate one way or the other, and found the following [11]:

> *"There definitely was a time when movement of Sun turned southward from the middle of asterism Āśleṣā, and northward from the beginning of Dhaniṣṭhā, because it has been said so in the earlier texts.*
>
> *Currently Sun turns southward from the beginning of Karkataka (Cancer) and turns other way from the beginning of Makara (Capricorn). If in the future there is deviation from this, then this should be ascertained by direct observation."*

The earlier text that Varāhamihira had in mind is the Vedāṅga Jyotiṣa, which says the following [12]:

> *"The Sun and the Moon turn towards the north at the first point of the Dhaniṣṭhā Nakṣatra, and towards the south at the middle point of Āśleṣā, and this always happens in the months of Māgha and Srāvaṇa."*

From the wordings of the verses, it is crystal clear that Varāhamihira is alluding to the phenomenon of the "Precession of the Equinoxes". It is related to the wobbling of the earth's axis, and has a period of about 26,000 years. As the zodiac has 12 signs, it takes approximately 2160 years to transit through one zodiac sign. If there is precession of the equinoxes, then it follows that there is precession of the solstices as well. The question then is -- when did the Sun turn southward from the beginning of Karkaṭaka (Cancer)?

According to Professor James B. Kaler of the University of Illinois, the date for the transition of the summer solstice into the next zodiac sign is the following [13]:

> *"As a result of precession, around 1990 the Summer Solstice crossed the modern boundary from Gemini to Taurus, which now technically holds the point. Because the Summer Solstice is closer to the classic figure of Gemini than it is to that of Taurus, and since Gemini (along with Pisces, Libra, and Sagittarius) quarters the ecliptic, Gemini is still traditionally taken as the Solstice's celestial home."*

Now that we know the Sun turned southward from the beginning of Gemini around 1990 CE and it takes about 2160 years to transit through one zodiac sign, we can calculate backwards and get the approximate dates for previous transitions. The results are illustrated in Figure 4.1 below, which shows zodiac signs with both western and Indian names. It was around 170 BCE that the summer solstice crossed the modern boundary from Cancer to Gemini.

Therefore, it was around this time that Varāhamihira was making his observation, which matches quite well his lifespan from 123 BCE to 41 BCE using the Śaka era of 550 BCE. If my calculation is right then the accepted date of Varāhamihira of 505 CE to 587 CE is invalidated.

Now, let's try to find out what was the approximate date of the earlier observation that Varāhamihira was referring to. These observations are in terms of Hindu asterisms (nakṣatras), so we need to map these asterisms to the zodiac signs. Fortunately, Varāhamihira himself has given us the tools to do that in a very simple manner. Varāhamihira says that the starting points of Aries (Meṣa) and Aśvinī asterism are the same [14]. With this information, the mapping of zodiacs to nakṣatras is shown in Figure 4.2. As the zodiacs divide the ecliptic, apparent path of the Sun in the background of stars, in 12, each zodiac spans for 30 degrees. There are 27 asterisms, so each asterism spans 13°20'.

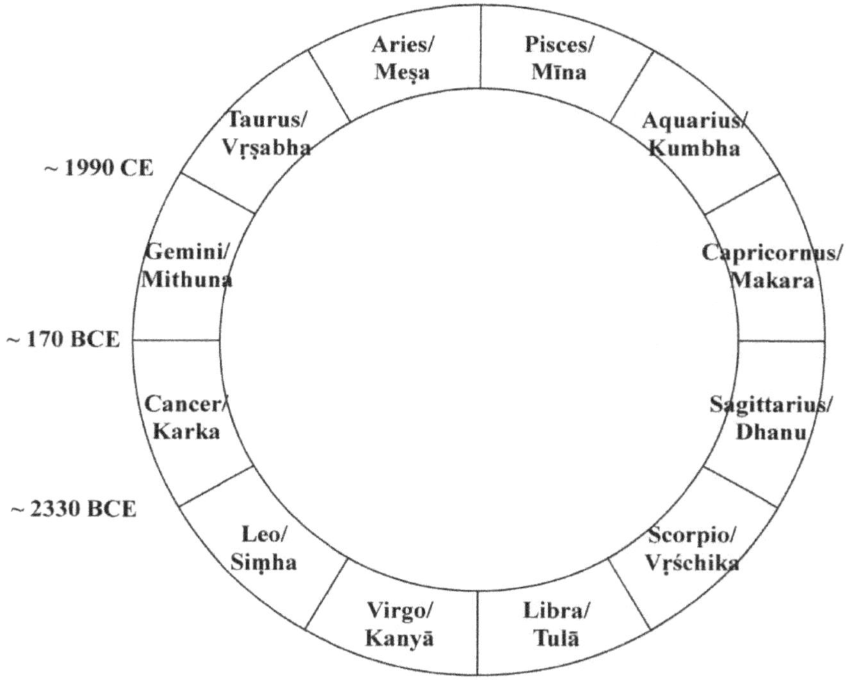

Figure 4.1: Transition of summer solstice into new Zodiac due to precession

As starting points of Aries and Aśvinī coincide, we get two more coincidences: 1) Starting points of Leo and Maghā; and 2) starting points of Sagittarius and Mūla. As the Sun turned southward from the beginning of Leo around 2330 BCE, it did so also from the beginning of Maghā, since the starting points of Leo and Maghā coincide. As each asterism spans 13°20' and it takes ~2160 years for the solstice to move through one zodiac of 30°, it will take ~960 years for the solstice to move through one asterism/nakṣatra.

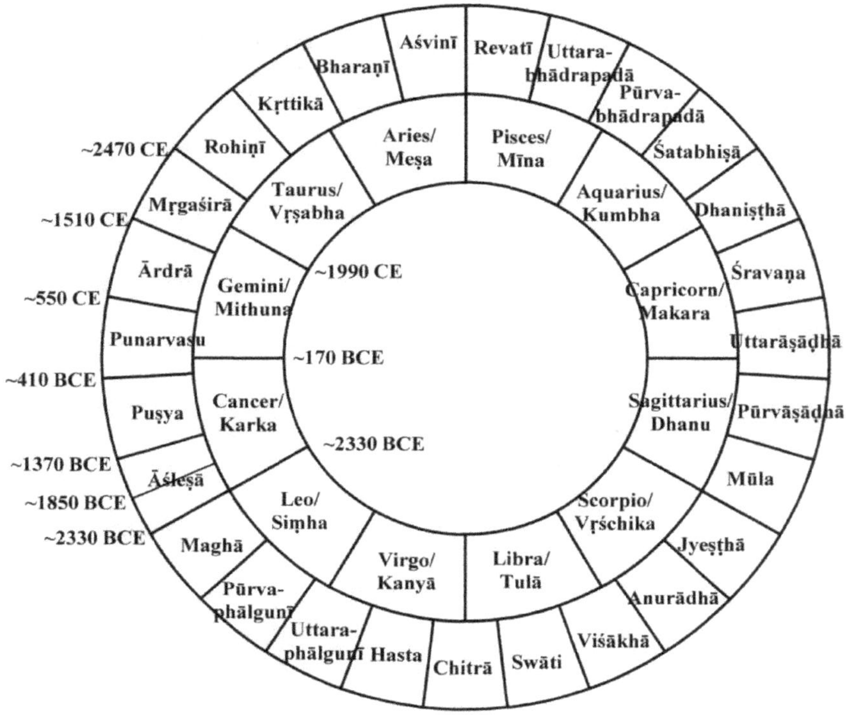

Figure 4.2: Transition of summer solstice into new asterism due to precession

Thus the Sun turned southward from the beginning of Āśleṣā around 1370 BCE and from the end of Āśleṣā (or beginning of Leo) around 2330 BCE. Taking the midpoint of these two dates, the Sun turned southward from the middle of Āśleṣā around 1850 BCE. This then is the approximate date when the observation detailed in the Vedāṅga Jyotiṣa was made. As this date is too early for the Vedic people to be in India, according to modern chronology, modern texts claim that this observation took place around 1400 BCE [15].

There is another statement by Varāhamihira stating that the Sun changed its course from the middle of Āśleṣā earlier, but now that takes place in Punarvasu [16]. If we look at Figure 4.2, we find that the starting point of Cancer falls in Punarvasu (about 2/3rd from the beginning of Punarvasu), so Varāhamihira's statements are consistent.

There is one more major problem to be resolved before Varāhamihira can be given the due he deserves. This is the problem of Varāhamihira quoting Āryabhaṭa I [17]. Āryabhaṭa has given information about his birth in Āryabhaṭīya. Modern texts translate the relevant verse to mean that Āryabhaṭa was 23 years old in the year 3600 of the Kali era. Therefore he wrote the book Āryabhaṭīya in 499 CE and was born in 476 CE. Naturally, Varāhamihira has to be of a later date. First of all, there is doubt whether Āryabhaṭa was born in 476 CE or 522 CE. Commentator Someśvara (11th century CE) has interpreted the verse to mean that Āryabhaṭa was born 23 years after 3600 years of Kali era had passed [18].

> *"Strange to say, commentator Someśvara understands the verse to mean that 3623 years had elapsed of the Kali Yuga at the birth of Āryabhaṭa."*

If this is the correct interpretation, then Varāhamihira can't be referring to the Āryabhaṭa of sixth century CE born after he wrote Pañchasiddhāntikā. Let's suppose that the accepted version is true. Then Āryabhaṭa wrote his famous book in 499 CE in Kusumpura, which modern historians identify with Patna in Bihar, while Varāhamihira wrote his treatise in far away Ujjain in 505 CE. Could Āryabhaṭa have become so famous in a mere six years to be quoted by Varāhamihira? We are talking of an age 1500 years ago, when information travelled much more slowly and it took much longer to build one's reputation.

Fortunately, Al-Biruni (11th century) has done us a big favour by providing a solution to this problem. Here is what he has to say:

> *"In the book of Āryabhaṭa of Kusumapura we read that the mountain Meru is in Himavant, the cold zone, not higher than a*

> *yojana. In the translation, however, it has been rendered so as to express that it is not higher than Himavant by more than a yojana. This author is not identical with the elder Āryabhaṭa, but he belongs to his followers, for he quotes him and follows his example. I do not know which of these two namesakes is meant by Balabhadra." [19]*

> *"I have not been able to find anything of the books of Āryabhaṭa. All I know of him I know through the quotations from him given by Brahmagupta. The latter says in a treatise called Critical Research on the Basis of the Canons, that according to Āryabhaṭa the sum of the days of a caturyuga is 1377,917,500, i.e. 300 days less than according to Pulisa. Therefore Āryabhaṭa would give to a kalpa 1,590,540,840,000 days. According to Āryabhaṭa and Pulisa, the kalpa and caturyuga begin with midnight which follows after the day the beginning of which is the beginning of the kalpa, according to Brahmagupta. Āryabhaṭa of Kusumapura, who belongs to the school of the elder Āryabhaṭa, says in a small book of his on Al-ntf (?), that '1008 caturyugas are one day of Brahman. The first half of 504 caturyugas is called utsarpini, during which the sun is ascending, and the second half is called avasarpini, during which the sun is descending. The midst of this period is called sama, i.e. equality, for it is the midst of the day, and the two ends are called durtama (?).' " [20]*

These two statements clearly show that Āryabhaṭa of Kusumapura, who was born in 476 CE or 522 CE and whom we know as Āryabhaṭa I, was in reality Āryabhaṭa II. Varāhamihira refers to Āryabhaṭa I about whom we hardly know anything at this point. We can only say that he must have lived before the time of Varāhamihira (123 BCE to 41 BCE).

Now that I have shown that Varāhamihira lived between 2nd century BCE and the 1st century BCE and used a Śaka era of 550 BCE presumably named after Cyrus the Great of Persia, it is time to understand why he chose this era.

4.2 What is in a Name?

Sometimes a name says a lot, and in the case of Varāhamihira it indeed does so. Varāhamihira is a combination of two words -- "Varāha" and "Mihira". Varāha meaning wild boar is an incarnation of Lord Viṣṇu. Mihira is a corrupted form of Mithra, an ancient Persian God equivalent to the Vedic God Mitra. As the word Mihira is of Persian origin, it points to Varāhamihira's forefathers coming to India from Persia. This is further confirmed by Varāhamihira being called a "Śākadwīpī Brāhmaṇa" by commentator Bhaṭṭotpala.

According to Agnipurāṇa, Śakadwīpa or island of Śakas is inhabited by Maga Brahmins, who are sun-worshippers [21]. Varāhamihira has instructed that idols of the Sun should be installed by Maga Brahmins [22]. Varāhamihira has also told us that he was the son of Ādityadāsa, born in Kapitthaka and living in Avanti [23]. As the kingdom of Avanti had its capital at Ujjayinī (Ujjain), Varāhamihira lived in the place from where the legendary Emperor Vikramāditya ruled. Ujjain was also the most important place for astronomical learning in ancient India, and so it was natural for the most celebrated astronomer of his time to live there. His father's name Ādityadāsa means servant of the Sun, and his own name has the Sun (Mihira) as part of it. This lends credence to the belief that he was from the family of Sun worshippers.

According to Indian tradition, Maga Brahimns came from Persia. The equivalent term Magi priests are well known from Persian history. The Magi were official priests of Achaemenid kings. The question then is why did the ancestors of Varāhamihira migrate to India? Throughout history, wars have been a major cause of migration. I consider the invasion of Persia by Alexander the Great as the most likely cause of this migration. We now have an explanation of why Varāhamihira would introduce the Śaka era instituted in the name of Cyrus the Great, ruler of Persia. All we need then to complete our investigation is to show that an important event took place in 550 BCE during the reign of Cyrus the Great that was worthy of instituting an era.

4.3 Cyrus the Great

Of all the kings that have been given the coveted title of "The Great", I consider Cyrus the Great to be the most worthy of this title. Some kings have been given this title for being great conquerors, but I don't consider the wanton pursuit of self-glory and bringing unwanted bloodshed of epic proportions to innocent people as signs of greatness. Here was a king who really cared about his people, and his subjects adored him. He is credited with instituting the first charter of human rights. When he conquered Babylon in 539 BCE, his first actions were to free the slaves and declare that everyone had the right to choose their religion.

Cyrus succeeded to the throne in 559 BCE. He was not an independent ruler, and was subordinate to Media. In 550 BCE he conquered Media, declared himself an independent king, and founded the Achaemenid Empire. Here is a quote describing the timeline of ancient Persian empires [24]:

> *"The Median Empire (728-550 BC) controlled the northern shore of the Persian Gulf and the Gulf of Oman, but did not extend west of the Tigris; the Achaemenid Empire (550-330 BC) included Mesopotamia and its access to the sea and the Parthian Empire (247 BC-224 AD) dominated the Arabian coast right up to Qatar."*

We know that the Śaka era referred to by Varāhamihira was instituted to celebrate the founding of the Achaemenid Empire. It is also of critical importance to know that Varāhamihira defines the era as that of the Śaka king, while the later Śaka era is invariably described as starting with the end of the Śakas. Varāhamihira's Śaka king is a good king, while the Śaka king of Śālivāhana Śaka era is an enemy king who needed to be eliminated. Let's call this Śaka era introduced in India by Varāhamihira as the Cyrus Śaka era to distinguish it from the Śālivāhana Śaka era beginning in 78 CE.

With his Persian background, Varāhamihira was uniquely qualified to write an astronomical treatise called Pañchasiddhāntikā that would elucidate the astronomical schools of India as well as Greece. Western scholars have argued that Indians learnt astronomy from Greeks based on the works of Varāhamihira. Nothing can be further from the truth. Indian astronomy was completely indigenous and was far more accurate than its Greek counterpart.

4.4 Where do we go from here?

Once I convinced myself that Varāhamihira lived during the 2nd and 1st century BCE, I pondered the implications of this finding. It is well known that Varāhamihira was one of the nine gems in the court of the legendary emperor Vikramāditya. We still use the era called Vikrama Samvat starting in 57 BCE named after Vikramāditya. Modern historians deny the very existence of a historical king named Vikramāditya in 57 BCE, and they claim that this era was started by Azes. Similarly, we still use the Śālivāhana Śaka era starting in 78 CE that we believe was started by the Śālivāhana (Sātavāhana) king Gautamīputra Sātakarṇī on the occasion of uprooting the Śakas. Modern historians claim that this Śaka era was started by Kaniṣka. How did Azes change in the Vikrama Samvat and Kaniṣka in Śālivāhana? Were our ancestors fools or were they somehow duped? If modern historians were to pay close attention to the Indian ethos, they would have sought and found a more plausible explanation. They offer no proof whatsoever for their assertions, and we are expected to accept their assertions as Gospel just because they have had the privilege of writing our history. In this context, let us look at the following passage by Al-Biruni [25]:

"Hindus believe that there is no country but theirs, no nation like theirs, no kings like theirs, no religion like theirs, no science like theirs. They are haughty, foolishly vain, self-conceited, and stolid. They are by nature niggardly in communicating that which they know, and they take the greatest possible care to withhold it from men of another caste among their own people, still much more, of course, from any foreigner. According to their belief, there is no other country on earth but theirs, no other race of man but theirs, and no created beings besides them have any knowledge or science whatsoever. Their haughtiness is such that, if you tell them of any science or scholar in Khurasan and Persis, they will think you to be both an ignoramus and a liar."

Such proud people don't institute eras in the name of foreigners. Instead, they celebrated the occasions when foreign invaders were defeated by their kings, and they instituted eras in the names of the victorious leaders. Once I was convinced of the timing of Varāhamihira (123 BCE to 41 BCE), I noticed that 57 BCE, the beginning of the Vikrama era, falls between these dates. Indian tradition puts Varāhamihira in the court of Emperor Vikramāditya as one of the nine gems, and it is because of him being placed in the 6th century that the existence of Emperor Vikramāditya has been denied. Noted historian D.C. Sircar says the following about the tradition of nine gems in the court of Emperor Vikramāditya [26]:

"This tradition is absolutely worthless for historical purposes not only because there seems to be no trace of it in early literature but also because of the facts that, out of the nine, at least Varāhamihira lived in the sixth century A.D. and not in the first century B.C., which is the age of Vikramāditya according to the legends, and that there is hardly any reason to believe that all the nine worthies mentioned in the list of the jewels of Vikrama's court lived in the same age."

One of the nine gems was named Vetāla Bhaṭṭa after whom the Vetāla of Vikrama and Vetāla stories have been written. Distinguished poet Kālidāsa was another gem in his court. In Kālidāsa's work Jyotirvidābharaṇa, he claims to have written the work in 33 BCE. Another luminary in Vikramāditya's court, Harisvāmin, has given a date close to 57 BCE [27].

> *"Another case somewhat of this type is offered by Harisvāmin's commentary on the Śatapatha Brāhmaṇa, which is said to have been composed in Kali 3047 = 55 B.C., while the author hailing from Puṣkara, is stated to have been serving king Vikrama of Avanti as Dharmādhyakṣa in charge of charities."*

Thus, we have another luminary in the court of Emperor Vikramāditya who can be placed close to the date of 57 BCE. Modern historians have declared the whole text of Jyotirvidābharaṇa by Kālidāsa as forgery, dismissing whatever that doesn't fit their chronology as either an interpolation or a forgery.

Given this, I could infer the possibility of a real historical Emperor Vikramāditya in 57 BCE. Once we find the difference of over 600 years between the accepted and alternative date of Varāhamihira, it is a simple exercise in figuring out who the real Emperor Vikramāditya was. However, to bring the real Vikramāditya to his true historical time involved a much bigger challenge of figuring out the starting point of the Kṛta and Mālava eras. A rough starting point of Krita and Mālava eras can be worked out fairly easily based on the evidence of the Mandsaur inscription during the time of Kumāragupta I, but few would take it seriously in the absence of a clincher argument. Modern history asserts that all three eras – the Vikrama era, the Kṛta era, and the Mālava era -- were identical. It took me many years to find a logical explanation and understand why the Kṛta era is named Kṛta era. The details of my findings are presented in the companion to this book titled "India after Alexander: The Age of Vikramādityas".

While I was preoccupied with the puzzle of the Vikrama, Kṛta and Mālava eras, it became obvious to me that previous challenges to accepted history have failed because over the course of last two centuries, no one has come up with a satisfactory alternative to the identity of Devānāmpriya Priyadarśī, whom modern history identifies with Aśoka Maurya. Based on what I had figured out, I was convinced that this identification was wrong. Thus began my search for the real Devānāmpriya Priyadarśī, who had listed five Greek kings in his inscriptions. After figuring out the identity of the real Devānāmpriya Priyadarśī, I reasoned that I would be expected to present a detailed alternative chronology of Indian history and show that most, if not all, known facts fit this alternate chronology better than the accepted chronology. This is not an easy task.

With this background, it is now time to thoroughly investigate the two sheet anchors on which modern Indian history is pinned and see if we can loosen their grip on the modern historical accounts. We will start by weighing who deserves to be the Sandrokottos of Greek accounts -- Chandragupta Maurya, the founder of the Mauryan dynasty, or Chandragupta I, the emperor of the Imperial Gupta dynasty.

Notes:

1. Bṛhat Saṃhitā 13.3.
2. Cunningham (1883): 9.
3. Bṛhat Saṃhitā 13.2.
4. Cunningham (1883): 10.
5. Rājataraṅgiṇī 1.51.
6. Rājataraṅgiṇī 1.49.
7. Rājataraṅgiṇī 1.50.
8. Cunningham (1883): 11.
9. Venkatachelam (1953): 50.
10. Pañchasiddhāntikā 1.8.
11. Bṛhat Saṃhitā 3.1-2.
12. Yajus Vedāṅga Jyotiṣa, Verse 7.
13. http://stars.astro.illinois.edu/celsph.html. Last accessed on July 28, 2015.
14. Bṛhat Jātaka 1.4.
15. Kumar et al. (2013): 14.
16. Pañchasiddhāntikā 3.20-22.
17. Pañchasiddhāntikā 15.20.
18. Dāji (1865). Quote on page 406.
19. Sachau (1910): 246.
20. Sachau (1910): 370-371.
21. Agnipurāṇa 119.15-22.
22. Bṛhat Saṃhitā 60.19.
23. Bṛhat Jataka 28.9.
24. Cadene and Dumortier (2013): 10.
25. Sachau (1910): 23.
26. Sircar (1969): 120-121.
27. Sircar (1969): 125.

"Two fixed ideas can no more exist together in the moral world than two bodies can occupy one and the same place in the physical world."
- Alexander Pushkin

5. SANDROKOTTOS VS. SANDROKOTTOS

"The jurisprudence of the Hindus and Arabs being the field which I have chosen for my peculiar toil, you cannot expect that I should greatly enlarge your collection of historical knowledge; but I may be able to offer you some occasional tribute; and I cannot help mentioning a discovery which accident threw in my way, though my proofs must be reserved for an essay which I have destined for the fourth volume of your transactions. To fix the situation of that Palibothra (for there may have been several of the name) which was visited and described by Megasthenes, had always appeared a very difficult problem; for though it could not have been Prayaga; where no ancient metropolis ever stood, nor Canyacubja, which has no epithet at all resembling the word used by the Greeks; nor Gaur, otherwise called Lacshmanavati, which all know to be a town comparatively modern, yet we could not confidently decide that it was Pāṭaliputra, though names and most circumstances nearly correspond, because that renowned capital extended from the confluence of the Sone and the Ganges to the site of Patna, while Palibothra stood at the junction of the Ganges and Erannoboas, which the accurate M. D'Anville has pronounced to be the Yamuna; but this only difficulty was removed when I found in a classical

> *Sanscrit book, near 2000 years old, that Hiranyabahu, or golden-armed, which the Greeks changed into Erannoboas, or the river with a lovely murmur, was in fact another name for the Sona itself; though Megasthenes, from ignorance or inattention, has named them separately. This discovery led to another of greater moment; for Chandragupta, who, from a military adventurer, became, like Sandracottus, the sovereign of Upper Hindustan, actually fixed the seat of his empire at Pataliputra, where he received ambassadors from foreign princes; and was no other than that very Sandracottus who concluded a treaty with Seleucus Nicator; so that we have solved another problem, to which we before alluded, and may in round numbers consider the twelve and three hundredth years before Christ as two certain epochs between Rama, who conquered Silan a few centuries after the flood, and Vicramaditya, who died at Ujjayini fifteen-seven years before the beginning of our era."*

With these words in 1793 CE [1], Sir William Jones, President of the Asiatic Society, changed the course of modern Indian history. The identification of Sandrokottos of Greek accounts with Chandragupta Maurya was a momentous occasion in the construction of modern Indian history. This is how McCrindle has described this discovery [2]:

> *"The discovery that the Sandrokottos of the Greeks was identical with the Chandragupta who figures in the Sanskrit annals and the Sanskrit drama was one of great moment, as it was the means of connecting Greek with Sanskrit literature, and of thereby supplying for the first time a date to early Indian history, which had not a single chronological landmark of its own."*

Chandragupta has been called by various names by Greeks: Sandrokottos by Strabo, Sandrakottos by Pliny, Androkottos by Plutarch [3] and Sandrocottus by Justin [4]. Chandragupta Maurya, the founder of the Mauryan Dynasty, is not the only candidate for identification as Sandrokottos. There is another Chandragupta, the emperor of the Imperial Gupta Dynasty, who also deserves serious consideration. Traditional Indian sources place Chandragupta Maurya during second millennium BCE, while modern history places Chandragupta Maurya during the period Alexander invaded the frontiers of India in 326 BCE. In the framework of the currently accepted chronology, Chandragupta I of the Gupta Dynasty is placed more than six centuries after Alexander's invasion, while traditional Indian sources place Chandragupta Maurya over twelve centuries before Alexander's invasion. Let's then go to the original sources and weigh the evidence to decide which Chandragupta was the Sandrokottos that the Greeks encountered.

5.1 The Predecessor of Sandrokottos

Greek classical writers Diodorus and Curtius respectively have named Xandrames or Agrammes as the ruler of India before Sandrokottos as follows:

> *"He had obtained from Phegeus a description of the country beyond the Indus: First came a desert which it would take twelve days to traverse; beyond this was the river called the Ganges which had a width of thirty-two stadia, and a greater depth than any other Indian river; beyond this again were situated the dominions of the nation of the Praisioi and the Gandaridai, whose king, Xandrames, had an army of 20,000 horse, 200,000 infantry, 2000 chariots, and 4000 elephants trained and equipped for war. Alexander, distrusting these statements, sent for Poros and questioned him as to their accuracy. Poros assured him of the correctness of the information, but added that the king of the Gandaridai was a man of quite worthless character, and held in no respect, as he was thought to be the son of a barber. This man-the king's father-was of a comely person, and of him the queen had become deeply enamoured. The old king having been treacherously murdered by his wife, the succession had devolved on him who now reigned." [5]*

"Next came the Ganges, the largest river in all India, the farther bank of which was inhabited by two nations, the Gangaridae and the Prasii, whose king Agrammes kept in the field for guarding the approaches to his country 20,000 cavalry and 200,000 infantry, besides 2000 four-horsed chariots, and, what was the most formidable force of all, a troop of elephants which he said ran up to the number of 3000.

All this seemed to the king to be incredible, and he therefore asked Porus, who happened to be in attendance, whether the account was true. He assured Alexander in reply that, as far as the strength of the nation and kingdom was concerned, there was no exaggeration in the reports, but that the present king was not merely a man originally of no distinction, but even of the very meanest condition. His father was in fact a barber, scarcely staving off hunger by his daily earnings, but who, from his being not uncomely in person, had gained the affections of the queen, and was by her influence advanced to too near a place in the confidence of the reigning monarch. Afterwards, however, he treacherously murdered his sovereign; and then, under the pretence of acting as guardian to the royal children, usurped the supreme authority, and having put the young princes to death begot the present king, who was detested and held cheap by his subjects, as he rather took after his father than conducted himself as the occupant of a throne." [6]

As Curtius, who uses the name Agrammes, belonged to the first century CE, and Diodorus, who uses the name Xandrames, belonged to the first century BCE, it is obvious that Xandrames is the original name, which has been corrupted into Agrammes. Xandrames has been identified by modern historians as the last ruler of the Nanda Dynasty. However, there is no phonetic similarity between the names of Nanda rulers and Xandrames or Agrammes, and it is obvious that this identification is a direct consequence of the identification of Sandrokottos with

Chandragupta Maurya. Therefore Greek sources do not support the view that Nandas were ruling India during Alexander's invasion.

5.2 The Successor of Sandrokottos

Greek classical writers have named Amitrochates or Allitrochades as the ruler of India after Sandrokottos as follows:

> *"Strabo (II.I.9) says: "Both of these men were sent as ambassadors to Palimbothra, - Megasthenes to Sandrokottus, Deimachus to Allitrochades, his son; and such are the notes of their residence abroad, which, I know not why, they thought fit to leave." "[7]*

> *"The Nanda dynasty which was supplanted by the Mauryan in 315 B.C. had succeeded to that of Sisunaga in 370 B.C. Its last member; whom the Greeks call Xandrames and Curtius Agrammes, is variously named in native writings Dhanananda, Nanda MahaPadma, and Hiranyagupta. Xandramas (of which Agrammes seems to be a distorted form) transliterates the Sanskrit Chandramas, which means Moon-god. A Hindu play - the Mudra Rakshasa-produced early in the Mahommedan period refers to the revolution by which Chanakya raised Chandragupta to power, but is of no historical value. Chandragupta was succeeded by his son Vindusara, who is called by Strabo Allitrochades, and by Athenaios (xiv. 67), Amitrochates, a form which transliterates the Sanskrit Amitraghata, a title by which he was frequently designated, and which means enemy-slayer." [8]*

First of all, the terms Allitrochades and Amitrochates don't match Bindusāra, son and successor of Chandragupta Maurya, by any stretch of the imagination. Modern history books teach that Bindusara used the title Amitraghāta ("Slayer of enemies"), the phonetic equivalent of Amitrochates, which is a pure lie. There is no evidence to this effect. Amitrochates, the name of the successor of Sandrokottos, is phonetically equivalent to the term "Amitrochchhetā" ("Mower of enemies"), which reminds us of the term "Sarvarājochchhetā" ("Mower of all kings") applied to

Samudragupta by his successors [9]. But why would Samudragupta introduce himself as Amitrochchhetā to the Greeks instead of his usual title Sarvarājochchhetā? The answer lies in the meaning of these two terms themselves. Samudragupta had adopted the title Sarvarājochchhetā ("Mower of all kings"), after physically eliminating most of the kings who lost the battle against him. Since Samudragupta did not eliminate Seleucus and instead married his daughter, this title did not fit the circumstances. Therefore, he introduced himself as Amitrochchhetā ("Mower of the enemies") reminding the Greeks that enmity with him was going to prove very costly.

5.3 Sandrokottos, the Person Himself

We have seen that the names of the predecessor and the successor of Sandrokottos do not match the predecessor and the successor of Chandragupta Maurya. Let's now analyze the information about Sandrokottos himself as provided by Greek classical writers.

5.3.1 Family name

We have the following information about the family name of Sandrokottos from the Greek classical writer Strabo [10]:

> *"The king in addition to his family name must adopt the surname of Palibothros, as Sandrokottus, for instance did, to whom Megasthanes was sent on an embassy."*

We do not know the surname of Palibothros, but the most likely intent of the passage was that the name Sandrokottos contained the family name of Sandrokottos. If Sandrokottos was Chandragupta Maurya then this will not hold. However, if Sandrokottos was Chandragupta of the Imperial Gupta Dynasty, then this will fit perfectly as "Gupta", which still is a popular family name in India, was part of the first name of all Imperial Gupta emperors such as Śrīgupta, Ghaṭotkachagupta, Chandragupta I, Samudragupta,

Chandragupta II, Kumāragupta, Purugupta, Skandagupta and Budhagupta.

5.3.2 Marriage Alliance

Greek classical writer Strabo says the following about Seleucus Nikator and Sandrokottos [11]:

> *"The Indus runs in a parallel course along the breadth of these regions. The Indians possess partly some of the countries lying along Indus, but these belonged formerly to the Persians. Alexander took them away from the Arianoi and established in them colonies of his own. Seleukos Nikator gave them to Sandrokottus in concluding a marriage alliance, and received in exchange 500 elephants."*

Modern historians claim that Seleucus Nikator gave his daughter in marriage to Chandragupta Maurya due to his defeat in the war. This is a direct consequence of the identification of Sandrokottos with Chandragupta Maurya. There is no corroborative evidence for this. In contrast, there is corroborative evidence for the marriage alliance in favour of the identification of Sandrokottos with Chandragupta I of the Imperial Gupta Dynasty. The son of Chandragupta I was Samudragupta, who was married to Dattadevī. The first part of the name "Datta" means "given", as in given due to defeat in war. The second part Devī is simply an honourable name for a woman. Thus Dattadevī was the name given after marriage. Samudragupta claims to have earned her using his prowess in the Eran Stone Inscription as quoted below [12]:

> *"(L. 9.)— . . . there was Samudragupta, equal to (the gods) Dhanada and Antaka in (respectively) pleasure and anger; . . . by policy; (and) [by whom] the whole tribe of kings upon the earth was [overthrown] and reduced to the loss of the wealth of their sovereignty;—*
>
> *(L. 13.)— [Who], by . . . satisfied by devotion and policy and valour,—by the glories, consisting of the consecration by*

> *besprinkling, &c., that belong to the title of 'king,'— (and) by . . . combined with supreme satisfaction, — . . . (was) a king whose vigour could not be resisted;—*
>
> *(L. 17.)— [By whom] there was married a virtuous and faithful wife, whose dower was provided by (his) manliness and prowess; who was possessed of an abundance of [elephants] and horses and money and grain; who delighted in the houses of . . . ; (and) who went about in the company of many sons and sons' sons;—*
>
> *(L. 21.)— Whose deeds in battle (are) kindled with prowess; (whose) . . . very mighty fame is always circling round about; and whose enemies are terrified, when they think, even in the intervals of dreaming, of (his). . . that are vigorous in war;"*

This will make perfect sense for a marriage alliance as a result of success in war. We know that Sandrokottos had an encounter with Alexander prior to Alexander's war with King Porus in 326 BCE. The war between Sandrokottos and Seleucus took place in circa 304 BCE. As Chandragupta will a middle-aged man at this time and Samudragupta a young man, the daughter of Seleucus was married to Samudragupta.

5.3.3 Mentor

It is well known that Chandragupta Maurya was installed as the ruler of Magadha by his mentor Chāṇakya, who engineered a coup to depose the last Nanda ruler. Chāṇakya then played a larger than life role as the Prime Minister of Chandragupta, his son Bindusāra, and grandson Aśoka. If Chandragupta Maurya was the Sandrokottos of Greek accounts, then the absence of any mention of Chāṇakya in the Greek accounts is difficult to explain.

5.4 The Coinage

The coinage used by Mauryan rulers was vastly different from the ones used by the Imperial Gupta rulers. Mauryan rulers were using punch-marked coins as quoted below [13]:

> *"The coins in circulation during the Mauryan period are known as punch-marked coins which neither bear the name of any of the Mauryan rulers nor do they carry any date. Most of these coins have only symbols like tree-in-railing, sun, moon, mountain, animals, birds, etc., punched or stamped on them."*

Imperial Gupta rulers are said to have issued gold coins due to earlier rule of Bactrian Greeks as described below [14]:

> *"It is the Bactrian Greeks who first introduced coins with names and portraits of the rulers who issued them. The figure of the king on the obverse and of a deity or other symbols on the reverse are executed with a high degree of artistic skill. Not only the other foreign hordes who invaded India, but even the Indian rulers adopted the system and issued coins of similar type, though the execution is much inferior. The Imperial Guptas issued a series of fine gold coins which, though inferior to those of the Greeks, are yet of high artistic standard."*

The question is, if Maurya rulers were contemporaries of Bactrian Greeks, why did they not issue gold coins? They were supposed to be in good contact as DevānāmpriyaPriyadarśī, whom historians have identified as Aśoka Maurya, had sent his missionaries to even farther away places like Macedonia and Egypt. However, not only the Mauryan rulers, but long after them the Śuṅga and Kaṇva rulers kept using the punch-marked coins as shown below [15]:

> *"Magadha issued coinage that may be called India's first national currency which was given the title of imperial type of punch marked coins. Magadha's rule from Pāṭaliputra was followed by that of Nanda, Maurya, Sunga and Kanva dynasties, and all of these dynasties issued punch marked coins of the imperial type."*

The conclusion is obvious. Maurya, Śuṅga and Kaṇva dynasties did not issue the gold coins because this technology was unknown to them as their time was several centuries earlier than the time of Bactrian Greeks.

5.5 The Severe Famine

According to Jain sources, there was a great famine during the rule of Chandragupta Maurya [16]:

> *"Traditional accounts celebrate the place, as the one whereto Bhadrabahu, known as the last Sruttakevalin and preceptor or spiritual guru of Emperor Chandragupta Maurya (321-296 BC) resorted to, leading thousands of lay followers, when the country around Pāṭaliputra had fallen under severe and prolonged famine condition. As such, he advised Chandragupta Maurya to make suitable arrangements for mobilization of people, and his Jain sangha, from famine-stricken region, to a safer place."*

However, according to the Greek classical writer Diodorus, India had never experienced a famine [17]:

> *"It is accordingly affirmed that famine has never visited India, and that there has never been a general scarcity in the supply of nourishing food...But, further, there are usages observed by the Indians which contribute to prevent the occurrence of famine among them; for whereas among other nations it is usual, in the contests of war, to ravage the soil, and thus to reduce it to an uncultivated waste, among the Indians, on the contrary, by whom husbandmen are regarded as a class that is sacred and inviolable, the tillers of the soil, even when battle is raging in their neighbourhood, are undisturbed by any sense of danger, for the combatants on either side in waging the conflict make carnage of each other, but allow those engaged in husbandry to remain quite unmolested. Besides, they neither ravage an enemy's land with fire, nor cut down its trees."*

If Sandrokottos was Chandragupta Maurya, Greek writers would have known about the severe famine and would not have written that famine had never visited India.

5.6 The List of Kings

Greek classical writers have noted that there were 153 kings between Father Bacchus and Alexander the Great or Dionysos and Sandrokottos, as shown below:

> *"Their kings from Father Bacchus down to Alexander the Great are reckoned at 153 over a space of 6451 years and three months." [18]*

> *"Father Bacchus was the first who invaded India, and was the first of all who triumphed over the vanquished Indians. From him to Alexander the Great 6451 years are reckoned with 3 months additional, the calculation being made by counting the kings who reigned in the intermediate period, to the number of 153." [19]*

> *"From the time of Dionysos to Sandrakottos the Indians counted 153 kings and a period of 6042 years, but among these a republic was thrice established…and another to 300 years, and another to 120 years. The Indians also tell us that Dionysos was earlier than Herakles by fifteen generations, and that except him no one made a hostile invasion of India, not even Kyros the son of Kambyses, although he undertook an expedition against the Skythians, and otherwise showed himself the most enterprising monarch in all Asia; but that Alexander indeed came and overthrew in war all whom he attacked, and would even have conquered the whole world had his army been willing to follow him." [20]*

Sethna has tabulated the list of kings, but there are only 111 kings starting from Svāyambhūva Manu, the first king in Indian lists, to Chandragupta Maurya, while there are 146 kings, starting from Svāyambhūva Manu to Chandragupta I [21]. Even though we don't exactly know who the Greeks had in mind when they talked about Father Bacchus or Dionysos, the evidence is clearly against

Chandragupta Maurya and in favor of Chandragupta I of the Imperial Gupta Dynasty being the contemporary of Alexander.

5.7 Traditional Indian History

There is an inconsistency in the Purāṇas as to the exact number of years that passed between the birth of Parīkṣita (shortly after the Mahābhārata war) and the coronation of Mahāpadmananda or Mahānanda, king of the Nanda Dynasty. The variations are 1015, 1050 or 1500 years. However, 1500 years seems to be the right number intended by the authors of the Purāṇas, as they also allocate 1000 years to the dynasty of Bṛhdratha, 138 years to the dynasty of Pradyota, and 362 years to the dynasty of Śiśunāga since the Mahābhārata war, which adds up to 1500 years [22]. Counting from 3138 BCE as the date of the Mahābhārata war, we get ~1638 BCE for the coronation of Mahāpadmananda. As the Nandas ruled collectively for 100 years, according to the Purāṇas, Chandragupta Maurya started his rule ~1538 BCE. Thus, according to traditional Indian history, Chandragupta Maurya could not have been the contemporary of Alexander the Great.

5.8 Empires: One too many

If Chandragupta Maurya was Alexander's contemporary, then his predecessor – the last Nanda emperor -- was ruling over North India when Alexander attacked Porus. According to the Purāṇas, the Nandas were sole monarchs of their time [23]:

> *"As son of Mahānandin by a Śūdra women will be born a king, Mahāpadma (Nanda), who will exterminate all kṣatriyas. Thereafter kings will be of Śūdra origin. Mahāpadma will be sole monarch, bringing all under his sole sway."*

Since the last of the Nanda rulers was ruling over all of North India at the time of Alexander's invasion, Greek historians should have described a unified North India. On the contrary, they mention two important rulers, one of Prasii and the other of Gangaridai, as mentioned below [24]:

> *"Next came the Ganges, the largest river in all India, the farther bank of which was inhabited by two nations, the Gangaridae and the Prasii, whose king Agrammes kept in the field for guarding the approaches to his country 20,000 cavalry and 200,000 infantry, besides 2000 four-horsed chariots, and, what was the most formidable force of all, a troop of elephants which he said ran up to the number of 3000."*

5.9 The Search for Palibothra

We now arrive at a very crucial part of the investigation, which is the identification of Palibothra, the city from where Sandrokottos ruled, according to classical Greek writers [25]:

> *"At the confluence of this river with another (the Erannoboas) is situated Palibothra, a city 80 stadia in length and 15 in breadth. It is of the shape of a parallelogram, and is surrounded by a wooden wall, pierced with loopholes for the discharge of arrows. It has a ditch in front for the purpose of defence and for receiving the sewage of the city. The people in whose country this place is situated are the most distinguished in all India, and are called the Prasioi."*

Palibothra has been identified by modern historians with modern day Patna in Bihar, but there is far more to it than we can understand at first glance. Let us explore in detail the various cities that have been identified with Palibothra by different researchers in the past.

5.9.1 Patna

Pāṭaliputra, the ancient name of Patna, matches Palibothra phonetically. We have the following details of the location of Palibothra provided by Megasthenes [26]:

> *"India is bounded on the north by the extremities of Tauros, and from Ariana to the Eastern Sea by the mountains which are variously called by the natives of these regions Parapamisos, and Hemodos, and Himaos, and other names, but by the Macedonians Kaukasos. The boundary on the west is the river Indus, but the southern and eastern sides, which are both much greater than the others, run out into the Atlantic Ocean. The shape of the country is thus rhomboïdal, since each of the greater sides exceeds its opposite side by 3000 Stadia, which is the length, of the promontory common to the south and the east coast, which projects equally in these two directions. [The length of the western side, measured from the Kaukasian mountains to the southern sea along the course of the river Indus to its mouths, is said to be 13,000 stadia, so that the eastern side opposite, with the addition of the 3000 stadia of the promontory, will be somewhere about 16,000 stadia. This is the breadth of India where it is both smallest and greatest.] The length from west to east, as far as Palibothra can be stated with greater certainty, for the royal road which leads to that city has been measured by schoeni, and is in length 10,000 stadia. The extent of the parts beyond can only be conjectured from the time taken to make voyages from the sea to Palibothra by the Ganges, and may be about 6000 stadia. The entire length, computed at the shortest, will be 16,000 stadia. This is the estimate of Eratosthenes, who says he derived it principally from the authoritative register of the stages on the Royal Road."*

From this description, we gather that Palibothra was at a distance of 10,000 stadia from the Indus River and 6000 stadia from the mouth of Ganges as estimated by Eratosthenes. The length of a stadium varied depending on the time and place. It was 157.5 meters for the Eratosthenian stadium, 185 meters for the Olympic stadium, and 210 meters for the Ptolemaic or Royal stadium [27]. Since the measurement is attributed to Eratosthenes, the use of Eratosthenian stadium is warranted. This will make Palibothra at 1,575 kilometers from Indus and 945 kilometers from the mouth of

Ganges. Of course, we do not know where on Indus this measurement is taken from. At that time, the most used travel route from present day Afghanistan to India was along Uttarāpatha, literally meaning Northern Highway. Some present-day towns along ancient Uttarāpatha are Kabul (ancient Kubhā), Peshawar (ancient Puruṣapura), Taxila (ancient Takṣaśilā), Lahore (ancient Lavapurī), Delhi (ancient Indraprastha, medieval Ḍhillī), Allahabad (ancient Prayāga), and Patna (ancient Pāṭaliputra). Uttarāpatha, the predecessor of the Grand Trunk Road ended at Tamluk (ancient Tāmralipti), close to the Bay of Bengal. Taxila is close to the Indus and can be taken as the point from where the measurement was made. The aerial distance between Taxila and Patna is ~1500 kilometer [28]. This is the shortest distance and the distance by road can be quite longer than this. We can estimate the distance by road along Uttarāpatha as follows [29]:

Taxila to Lahore: ~380 km
Lahore to Delhi: ~450 km
Delhi to Allahabad: ~660 km
Allahabad to Patna: ~370 km

Thus the estimated distance between Taxila to Patna is ~1860 km, which is greater than 1575 km.

According to Megasthenes, the estimated distance of 945 km from Palibothra to the mouth of the Ganges is based on the time taken by voyage along the Ganges. A present day town close to the mouth of the Padma River, the main distributary of the Ganges, is Bhola in Bangladesh. The aerial distance between Patna, India and Bhola, Bangladesh is ~650 kilometers [28]. I have tried below to estimate the distance between Patna and Bhola along the Ganges by choosing cities on the banks of the Ganges [29]:

Patna, India to Bhagalpur, India: ~230 km
Bhagalpur, India to Farakka, India: ~160 km
Farakka, India to Ishwardi, Bangladesh: ~190 km

Ishwardi, Bangladesh to Rajbari, Bangladesh: ~100 km
Rajbari, Bangladesh to Bhola, Bangladesh: ~260 km

The estimated total distance between Patna and Bhola is ~940 km, which is very close to the distance of 945 km reported by Megasthenes. Thus these measurements support the identification of Palibothra as modern day Patna. Let's now look at other potential identifications for Palibothra.

5.9.2 Bhagalpur

Not many people know that at one time Bhagalpur was also considered to be the Palibothra of Greek writers. The case for the modern day Bhagalpur being the Palibothra was made by William Francklin as follows [30]:

> *"I now proceed to compare the distance assigned by Pliny, from the conflux of the Jumna with the Ganges to the site of Palibothra and thence to the sea, with the relative position, in those respects, of modern Bhagulpoor; hoping, if my comparison be correct, to add another link to the chain of my reasoning in favour of this site. In Pliny's Natural history, (book vi, chapter 17), we find mention of the following places, said to have been visited by Seleucus Nicator during his inroad into India.*
>
> > 'The remainder of the places," says Pliny, "visited by king Seleucos Nicator were as follows. To the river Hesidrus 168 miles; as much more to the Jomanes river; from thence to the Ganges, 112 miles. To Rodopham, 119 miles (others assign to this spot the distance of 325). To the city of Calinipaxa, 167 (others 265 miles); thence to the confluence of the Jumna and Ganges, 725 miles; thence to Palibothra, 425 miles; and again, from the conflux to the sea or mouth of the Ganges, 738 miles.'
>
> *Now I should conceive that the latter part of this statement, concerning the distance from the conflux of the Ganges to Jumna,*

being, first, to Palibothra four hundred and twenty five miles, and secondly, from the conflux to the sea, seven hundred and fifty eight miles, will nearly correspond with the actual situation of Bhagulpoor and Colgong, and with Injelly and the island of Saugor, at the present day. The distance from Allahabad to Bhagulpoor is about three hundred and fifty two British miles, according to the following computation in miles and Hindostany coss, reckoning at two miles the coss. ...If then we take three hundred and fifty two miles to Bhagulpoor, and add twenty to Colgong, which I suppose to be the eastern boundary of Palibothra General, and from thence six miles to Patergotah, opposite the confluence of the Cosi and the Ganges, we shall have from Allahabad to Palibothra a distance of three hundred and seventy eight British miles, to correspond with the four hundred and twenty-five Roman miles of Pliny. Pliny has been accused by some of forming erroneous ideas of geographical distances; but I am of opinion, that in the present instance, he has borne himself through.

Pliny reckons six thousand stadia from the conflux of the Jumna and Ganges to the sea, which being divided by eight, will give seven hundred and fifty miles, agreeing nearly with the present distance from Allahabad to Sagor. If these distances be found correct, a very fair argument is deducible from them: - we approach nearer to the geographic site of Palibothra than any others have done before us.

The Allahabad could not have been this famous city, is evident, I think, from the distance assigned by Pliny from the conflux of the Jumna and Ganges, first to Palibothra, and then to the sea. It has been argued, from the resemblance of the word Puraug, the Sanscrit name for Allahabad, that that place was the capital of the Prasii; but the word Puraug I understand to imply remission of sins, and here it alludes to the efficacy of the holy waters at that place, derived from the triple union of the Ganges, of the Jumna, and of the Seresooty or Serswatty, the latter of which is not visible; the place is thence denominated Trebanse, or the Triple Alliance, in evident allusion, as I think to the Indian Triad, which is the basis of their mythology. Neither could Kanouj have been the place, for the reasons assigned above, with the exception of the latitude. Neither, in my opinion, could it have been Patna, or any place in its vicinity, at the junction of the Ganges and the Soan; for where is the Erranaboas of the Greeks? Or the Cosi, the Cosike of the Hindoos? Or where are the hills, in the neighbourhood of which it is described as situated? There are none within many miles of Patna, whilst at Bhaugulpoor and its neighbourhood, both to the south and west, and to Colgong eastward, they are to be seen in abundance."

The argument rests on these two distances mentioned by Pliny:

1. Palibothra was at a distance of 425 miles from the confluence of the Jumna and Ganges.
2. Sea or mouth of the Ganges was at 738 miles from the confluence.

Allahabad is at the confluence of the Yamuna and the Ganges. The distance between Allahabad and Patna is ~370 km and the distance between Patna and Bhagalpur is ~230 km, so the distance between Allahabad and Bhagalpur is 600 km. One Roman mile is equal to 1.48 km, and so the distance between Allahabad and Patna is ~250 Roman miles, and the distance between Patna and Bhagalpur is ~155 Roman miles. Thus, the distance between Allahabad and Bhagalpur is ~405 Roman miles. This matches very well with the location of Bhagalpur as Palibothra of the Greeks at a distance of 425 Roman miles from the confluence of the Yamuna and Ganges. Next, Pliny specifies 738 Roman miles or 1092 km for the distance between the confluence and the sea or mouth of the Ganges. William Francklin takes the island of Sagar as the mouth of the Ganges and thinks that the distance between the confluence (of the Ganges and Yamuna) and the island of Sagar matches the distance given by Pliny. The island of Sagar is at the mouth of the Hooghly River, which is a minor distributary of the Ganges. It is more likely that the Greeks meant a major distributary like the Padma instead of the Hooghly, when they talked about the mouth of the Ganges.

Regardless, I have estimated below the distance between Allahabad and the island of Sagar along the Ganges and Hooghly [29].

Allahabad to Patna: ~370 km
Patna to Bhagalpur: ~230 km
Bhagalpur to Farakka: ~160 km
Farakka to Murshidabad: ~90 km
Murshidabad to Kolkata: ~240 km
Kolkata to Noorpur: ~ 60 km
Noorpur to Sagar: ~ 100 km

The estimated total distance between Allahabad to Sagar is ~1250 km. The estimated total distance between Allahabad, India and Bhola, Bangladesh on the other hand is ~1300 km. Both of these estimated distances are greater than 1092 km reported by Pliny, but reasonable considering the circumstances nearly two millennia ago.

We are now left with two more candidates for Palibothra -- Prayāga and Kannauj. Let's explore the possibility of Prayāga being the Palibothra of the Greeks next.

5.9.3 Prayāga

The idea of Prayāga, present day Allahabad, being the Palibothra of the Greeks is based on the statement of Arrian and Pliny as follows:

> *"Pliny (lib. VI, c. xix) calls it the Jomanes, and states that it flows into the Ganges through the Palibothri, between the towns of Methora and Chrysobara (Krishnapura?)." [31]*
>
> *"The site of Palibothra is one main point in which, after much discussion, geographers have in vain endeavoured to form an unanimous opinion. It was found by Magasthenes the proud capital of the Gangetic kingdom, and the greatest of all India. Yet modern geographers have not been able to agree within several hundred*

> *miles upon this marked and celebrated position. Arrian states that it is situated at the junction of the Ganges with the Erranaboas, the third river of India as to magnitude, being surpassed only by the Ganges and the Indus. This scale of magnitude suggests the Jumna, and at the confluence of the Jumna with the Ganges actually stands Allahabad, a city of great magnitude and high antiquity, which is even revered by the Hindoos as the "king of holy cities." Upon this general idea d'Anville and, after him, Robertson, have considered Allahabad as occupying the site of Palibothra." [32]*

The statement by Pliny is clear that Palibothra is located where Yamuna flows into the Ganges. That place is Prayāga, and there can be no question about it. Regarding the statement by Arrian, Erranaboas has now been accepted as Hiraṇyabāhu, which was another name for Sone River. Although Megasthenes has listed Erranaboas and Sone separately, this is now considered an error on his part. Let us now explore the possibility of Kannauj being the Palibothra of the Greek writers.

5.9.4 Kannauj

The identification of Kannauj with Palibothra has been made by Rennell [33]:

> *"Strabo gives the distance of Palibothra above the mouth of the Ganges at 6000 stadia; and though we cannot fix the exact length of the stade, we can collect enough to understand that 6000 stades laid off from the mouth of the Ganges would not reach far, if at all, beyond Patna. Nor must we forget the passage of Arrian (in Indicis) in which Palibothra, the chief city of the Indians upon the Ganges, is said to lie towards the mouths of that river. But we ought not to omit, on the other hand, that Arrian quotes from Eratosthenes, the distance of Palibothra from the western extreme of India, which is said to be 10,000 stades, only: and that Ptolemy gives its latitude at 27°; both which particulars apply better to Canoge than to Patna. It is possible that both places may have been occasionally used as*

> *capitals of the Prasii, as we have known both Agra and Delhi to have been of Hindoostan in general, during the last two centuries."*

Rennell gives two reasons for Kannauj being Palibothra: 10,000 stadia from India's western border and at 27° latitude. We have seen earlier that 10,000 stadia are equal to 1,575 km. The distance between Kannauj and Taxila, on the western border of India as considered by Greeks, can be estimated as follows [29]:

> Taxila to Lahore: ~380 km
> Lahore to Delhi: ~450 km
> Delhi to Kannauj: ~400 km (via Mathura)

The estimated distance of Kannauj from Taxila by road is ~1230 km, which is much shorter than 1,575 km. However, the latitude of Kannauj is 27.07°N, which matches very well with the figure given by Ptolemy. In contrast, the latitude of Patna is 25.61°N. We cannot put too much confidence in this match though, as the numbers for latitude and longitude of Indian cities given by Ptolemy are not very accurate in general due to the state of science nearly two millennia ago. Further support for the identification of Kannauj with Palibothra comes from the correct identification of the Prasii kingdom, a discussion which I will take up next.

5.10 The Kingdom of Prasii

We have the following information from Megasthenes about Prasii, of which Palibothra was the capital:

> *"According to Megasthenes the mean breadth (of the Ganges) is 100 stadia, and its least depth 20 fathoms. At the meeting of this river and another is situated Palibothra, a city eighty stadia in length and fifteen in breadth. It is of the shape of a parallelogram, and is girded with a wooden wall, pierced with loopholes for the discharge of arrows. It has a ditch in front for defence and for receiving the sewage of the city. The people in whose country this city is situated is the most distinguished in all India, and is called the Prasii."* [34]

> *"But the Prasii surpass in power and glory every other people, not only in this quarter, but one may say in all India, their capital being Palibothra, a very large and wealthy city, after which some call the people itself the Palibothri,--nay even the whole tract along the Ganges. Their king has in his pay a standing army of 600,000 foot-soldiers, 30,000 cavalry, and 9,000 elephants: whence may be formed some conjecture as to the vastness of his resources." [35]*

The Prasii kingdom has been identified as Prāchya, meaning eastern region, by modern historians [36]:

> *"Prasiaca (Ptol. Vii.1.53), a very extensive and rich district in the centre of Hindostan, along the banks of the Ganges and the Sona, whose chief town was the celebrated Palibothra. The name of its inhabitants, which is written with slight differences in different authors, is most correctly given as Prasii by Strabo and by Plini, who states that their king supported daily no less than 150,000 foot, 30,000 horse, and 9000 elephants. Diodorus calls them Praesii (xvii.93), as does also Plutarch. In Curtius again they occur under the form of Pharrasii (ix.2.3). It was to the king of Prasii, Sandracottus (Chandragupta), that the famous mission of Megasthenes by Seleucos took place. All authors concur in stating that this was one of the largest of the Indian empires, and extended through the richest part of India, from the Ganges to the Panjab. There can be no doubt that Prasii is a Graecised form for the Sancrit Prachinas (meaning the dwellers in the east)."*

Prāchya means eastern, and thus seems fit to describe the region around Patna, which is towards the eastern part of India. However, Pāṭaliputra was the capital of Magadha, and there is no evidence whatsoever that Magadha was known as Prāchya during the time of Alexander's invasion, and a few centuries thereafter. We have seen that the identification of Palibothra, capital city of Prasii, itself is subject to controversy, so we need to investigate further which region of India was called Prasii by the Greeks. Greek writers have used many variations of this name, such as Prasioi, Prasii, Praisioi, Praiisioi, Bresioi, Pharrasii, Praesides and Praxiake [37]:

> *"The Sanskrit word Prāchyās (plur. of Prachya, "eastern") denoted the inhabitants of the east country, that is, the country which lay to the east of the river Sarasvati, now the Sursooty, which flows in a south-western direction from the mountains bounding the north-east part of the province of Delhi till it loses itself in the sands of the great desert. The Magadhas, it would seem, had, before Alexander's advent to India, extended their power as far as this river, and hence were called Prachyas by the people who lived to the west of it. They are called by Strabo, Arrian, and Pliny, Prasioi, Prasii; by Plutarch, Praisioi; by Nikolaos Damask., Praiisioi; by Diodoros, Bresioi; by Curtius, Pharrasii; by Justin, Praesides. Ailianos in general writes Praisioi like Plutarch, but in one passage where he quotes Megasthenes, he transcribes the name with perfect accuracy in the adjective form as Praxiake. General Cunningham does not agree in referring the name to Prāchya, as all the other modern writers do, but takes Prasii to be only the Greek form of Palāsiya or Parāsiya, a 'man of Palāsa or Parāsa,' a name of Magadha of which Palibothra was the capital. This derivation, he says, is supported by the spelling of the name given by Curtius, who calls the people Pharrasii, an almost exact transcript of Parāsiya (see his Ancient Geog. of India, p. 454). His view, we think, is hardly destined to supplant the other. Ptolemy describes in his Geography a small kingdom with seven cities which he locates in the regions of the upper Ganges, and calls Prasiake. Kanoge is one of these cities, but Palibothra is not in the number, appearing elsewhere as the capital of the Mandalai. One is at a loss to understand what considerations could have led Ptolemy to push the Prasians so far from their proper seats and transfer their capital to another people."*

However, we have the shocking disclosure from Ptolemy that during his time Palibothra was no longer a part of the kingdom of

Prasiake, but had become part of Mandalai. He lists Kannauj as the major city of Prasiake. Claudius Ptolemy lived between c. 90-150 CE and his writing reflects the condition of India during the early second century of the Christian era. Ptolemy mentions seven cities as part of Prasiake, and gives their co-ordinates as shown below in Table 5.1 [38]:

Table 5.1: Longitude and latitude of cities

Cities	**Longitude**	**Latitude**
Sambalaka	132°15'	31°50'
Adisdara	136°	31°30'
Kanagora	135°	30°40'
Kindia	137°	30°20'
Sagala, the east of the river	139°	30°20'
Aninakha	137°20'	31°40'
Koangka	138°20'	31°30'

McCrindle identifies Sambalaka as Sambhal, a town of Rohilkhand; Adisdara as Ahichhatra; Kanagora as Kannauj; Kindia as Kant, an ancient city of Rohilkhand and Shahjahanpur of the present ; Sagala as possibly Sakula or Kusinagara; Aninakha not identified, and Koangka as Kanaka with locality unknown [39]. What is striking is that all the cities that have been properly identified as part of Prasiake were part of the very ancient kingdom of Pañchāla. We also have mention of Pañchāla being part of Prāchya region by none other than Pāṇini [40]:

> *"Panini's geographical horizon extended to Kalinga in the east, to Sind and Cutch in the west, to Taxila and Asmaka in the north-west. He also refers to Prachya Janapadas, comprising Panchala, Videha, Anga and Vanga."*

In the light of information presented in this chapter, a new understanding emerges of the state of India during the time of Alexander's invasion and the period after the invasion. All the evidence presented shows that Chandragupta Maurya was not the contemporary of Alexander the Great. It was Chandragupta I of the Imperial Gupta Dynasty who was the contemporary of Alexander the Great. But we can go beyond this understanding by showing that Greeks have presented us with evidence for three capitals of the Imperial Gupta empire: Pāṭaliputra (Patna), Prayāga (Allahabad) and Kānyakubja (Kannauj). Bhagalpur does not seem like a serious contender. As the Magadha Empire grew out of present day Bihar and Jharkhand to include present day Uttar Pradesh, the capital was shifted from Pāṭaliputra to Prayāga to better govern the empire. As the empire grew further to include present day Punjab and beyond, the capital was shifted to Kānyakubja, further west of Prayāga. Megasthenes had made several visits to the court of Sandrokottos. The capital may have been shifted in between his visits. Megasthenes being a visitor to India might have thought that he had come to the same place resulting in the conflicting details of Palibothra.

We can now understand why Samudragupta's pillar is located at Allahabad. Contrary to the opinion of modern historians, Allahabad is the original location of Samudragupta's pillar. Not only that, it was originally erected by Samudragupta. The inscriptions of Devānāmpriya Priyadarśī were inscribed on it later. This single evidence is powerful enough to force historians to rewrite Indian history. To realize the goal of rediscovering/reconstructing the history of India, we will need to discover the real identity of Devānāmpriya Priyadarśī. This is the evidence on which all of Indian chronology rests and for which we have not found a satisfactory alternative explanation over the last 175 years. No doubt, this is a monumental challenge, and this is the challenge I will take up now so that we can discover the correct history of India.

Notes:

1. Jones (1793): xii-xiv.
2. McCrindle (1877): 7, Footnote.
3. McCrindle (1877): 10.
4. Justinus, Historiarum Philippicarum Libri XLIV, XV.4.19.
5. McCrindle (1893): 281-282.
6. McCrindle (1893): 221-222.
7. Hamilton (1892): 109.
8. McCrindle (1893): 409.
9. Sethna (1989): 246.
10. McCrindle (1901): 42-43.
11. McCrindle (1901): 88-89.
12. Fleet (1888): 20-21.
13. Agnihotry (2010): A-245.
14. Majumdar (1977): 218.
15. Bernholz and Valubel (2014): 54.
16. Subba Reddy (2009): 126.
17. McCrindle (1877): 32-33.
18. McCrindle (1901): 108.
19. McCrindle (1877): 115.
20. McCrindle (1877): 203-204.
21. Sethna (1989): 77-78.
22. Sethna (1989): 5.
23. Pargiter (1913): 69.
24. McCrindle (1893): 221-222.
25. McCrindle (1901): 42.
26. McCrindle (1877): 48-50.
27. Sarton (1993): 105.
28. Using Distance calculator by Daft Logic,

http://www.daftlogic.com/
29. Using Google Maps, http://www.google.ca/maps/
30. Francklin (1815): 42-46.
31. McCrindle (1885): 98.
32. Murray (1844): 46-47.
33. Rennell (1788): 53-54.
34. McCrindle (1877): 66-67.
35. McCrindle (1877): 139.
36. Smith (1873): 667.
37. McCrindle (1893): 365-366.
38. McCrindle (1885): 131-132.
39. McCrindle (1885): 131-135.
40. Sen (1999): 58.

"When one door closes, another door opens; but we so often look so long and regretfully upon the closed door, that we do not see the ones which open for us."

- Alexander Graham Bell

6. BELOVED OF THE GODS

"But the moment any name or event turns up in the course of such speculations offering a plausible point of connection between the legends of India and the rational histories of Greece and Rome, - a collision between the fortunes of an eastern and western hero, - forthwith a speedy and spreading interest is excited which cannot be satisfied until the subject is thoroughly sifted by the examination of all the ancient works, western and eastern, that can throw concurrent light on the matter at issue. Such was the engrossing interest which attended the identification of Sandracottus with Chandragupta in the days of Sir William Jones: ... The discovery I was myself so fortunate as to make, last year, of the alphabet of the Delhi pillar inscription, led immediately to results of hardly less consideration to the learned world. Dr. Mill regarded these inscriptions as all but certainly demonstrated relics of the classical periods of Indian literature. This slight remainder of doubt has been since removed by the identification of Piyadasi as Aśoka, which we also owe to Mr. Turnour's successful researches; ... I have now to bring to the notice of the Society another link of the same chain of discovery, which will, if I do not deceive myself, create a yet stronger degree of general interest in the labours, and of confidence in the deductions, of our antiquarian members than any that has preceded it. ... But the principal fact which arrests attention in this very curious proclamation, is its allusion to Antiochus the Yona,

(Sanskrit Yavana) or Greek king. ... Mr. Turnour fixes the date of Aśoka's accession in B.C. 247, or 62 years subsequent to Chandragupta, the contemporary of Seleucus. Many of his edicts are dated in the 28th year, that is in B.C. 219, or six years after Antiochus the Great had mounted the throne." [1]

"In continuation of the discovery I had the pleasure of bringing to the notice of the Society at its last meeting, I am now enabled to announce that the edicts in the ancient character from Gujerat do not confine their mention of Greek sovereigns to Antiochus the ally of Aśoka, but that they contain an allusion equally authentic and distinct, to one of the Ptolemies of Egypt! ... It seems therefore more rational to refer the allusion in our edict to the former period, and so far to modify the theory I have lately adopted on prima facie evidence of the treaty of Aśoka with Antiochus the Great, as to transfer it to the original treaty with one of his predecessors, the first or second of the same name, Soter or Theos, of whom the former may have the preference from his close family connection with both Ptolemy and Magas, which would readily give him the power of promising free communication between India and Egypt." [2]

With these words in his two papers presented to the Asiatic Society of Bengal in February and March 1838 CE, James Prinsep, Secretary of the Asiatic Society, fixed the second sheet anchor of modern Indian history. We note here that in the first paper Prinsep identified Antiochus III the Great as the contemporary of Aśoka, but changed to Antiochus I or II in the second paper just a month later. This has important bearing on the discussion to follow in this chapter. The identification of Devānāmpriya Priyadarśī of the inscriptions with Aśoka Maurya of the Mauryan dynasty is the most important sheet anchor of Indian history. It is this identification, which warrants Chandragupta Maurya to be the contemporary of Alexander the Great instead of Chandragupta of Imperial Gupta Dynasty. As Aśoka Maurya is made out to be the contemporary of five Greek rulers during the 3rd century BCE, there remains no doubt that the contemporary of Alexander and Seleucos was Chandragupta Maurya, grandfather of Aśoka Maurya, and not Chandragupta I of the Imperial Gupta Dynasty, who was posterior to Aśoka Maurya by several centuries.

Any attempt to rewrite Indian history will not succeed unless it can be shown that the identification of Devānāmpriya Priyadarśī of the inscriptions with Aśoka Maurya is wrong. As this problem is well understood, there have been several attempts in the past to provide alternative explanations. Before we go into the details of these alternatives, we need to first look at the thirteenth rock edict of Devānāmpriya Priyadarśī, which mentions the five Greek rulers supposed to be his contemporaries [3]:

> *"And this (conquest) has been won repeatedly by Devānāmpriya both here and among all (his) borderers, even as far as at (the distance of) six hundred yojanas, where the Yona king named Antiyoka (is ruling), and beyond this Antiyoka, (where) four-4-kings (are ruling), (viz. the king) named Turamaya, (the king) named Antikini, (the king) named Maka, (and the king) named Alikasudara, (and) towards the south, (where) the Chodas and Pāṇḍyas (are ruling), as far as Tāmrapaṃī."*

This is the piece of evidence on which the chronology of Indian history rests. Are the five Greek kings mentioned here really the same as the modern historians identify? Was Devānāmpriya Priyadarśī really Aśoka Maurya? It is time to find out.

6.1 The Insurmountable Challenge

We have these five Greek kings mentioned by Devānāmpriya Priyadarśī: Antiyoka, Turamaya, Antikini, Maka and Alikasudara. Their phonetic equivalents are Antiochus, Ptolemy, Antigonus, Magas, and Alexander respectively. Is there any alternative explanation than the one given by modern historians? Let's see what alternatives traditional historians have come up with so far:

Alternative explanation 1:

Devānāmpriya Priyadarśī is not Aśoka Maurya, but Aśokāditya, another name of Samudragupta. Pandit Kota Venkatachelam quotes Somayajulu as follows:

> *"The so-called inscriptions of Aśoka do not belong to Aśoka. Most of them do not make any mention of Aśoka. If one or two mention Aśoka they do not refer to Aśoka Vardhana of the Maurya dynasty but they refer to Samudragupta of the Gupta dynasty who assumed the title of Aśokāditya."* [4]

The problem with this explanation is that there is no evidence whatsoever that Samudragupta ever took the title Aśokāditya and therefore this identification cannot be taken seriously. Additionally, there is no match between the characters of Samudragupta and Devānāmpriya Priyadarśī.

Alternative explanation 2:

Antiyoka, Turamaya, Antikini, Maga and Alikasudara are not kings, but the names of regions on the frontiers of ancient India in second millennium BCE, the time of Aśoka Maurya according to traditional Indian chronology [5].

Apart from being unconvincing, there is a major problem with this explanation. In April 1958, a rock inscription was found at Shar-i-Kuna near Kandahar in Southern Afghanistan, which is a bilingual inscription in Greek and Aramaic. Prima facie, whoever Devānāmpriya Priyadarśī was, his time was after the invasion of India by Alexander, as this bilingual inscription presupposes the existence of Greek colonies on the frontiers of India. Sethna has presented a feeble explanation that the Greek part of the inscription is a much later addition to the original in Aramaic [6].

So, it seems that there is no way out of this complication. But with all the evidence to the contrary that I have presented in this book so far, there has got to be a sensible explanation. In order to get to that explanation and identify the real Devānāmpriya Priyadarśī, we will need to go back to the drawing board and think afresh. Do modern historians have it right? Is Devānāmpriya Priyadarśī really Aśoka Maurya? Let's find out by comparing Devānāmpriya Priyadarśī known from his inscriptions with Aśoka Maurya known from literature. For if both of them are one and the same then information from the inscriptions must match the information from literature.

6.2 Aśoka Maurya from Literature

There is plenty of literary information available about Aśoka Maurya. According to Prof. Basham, literary sources for the information on Aśoka are the following: 1. Chronicles of Sri Lanka; 2. Aśokāvadāna as preserved in Divyāvadāna and Chinese versions; 3. Records of Chinese pilgrims; 4. Rājataraṅgiṇī of Kalhaṇa; and 5. Purāṇas [7]. Chronicles of Sri Lanka include Dīpavanśa and Mahāvanśa, while records of Chinese pilgrims include travel notes of Fa-Hien and Yuan Xang. Let's get an idea of what Aśoka Maurya was like from the travel notes of Fa-Hien. I will supplement information from other sources as we go along.

> *"When king Aśoka, in a former birth, was a little boy and played on the road, he met Kasyapa Buddha walking. (The stranger) begged food, and the boy pleasantly took a handful of earth and gave it to him. The Buddha took the earth, and returned it to the ground on which he was walking; but because of this (the boy) received the recompense of becoming a king of the iron wheel, to rule over Jambudvipa. (Once) when he was making a judicial tour of inspection through Jambudvipa, he saw, between the iron circuit of the two hills, a naraka for the punishment of wicked men. Having thereupon asked his ministers what sort of a thing it was, they replied, "It belongs to Yama, king of demons, for punishing wicked people." The king thought within himself: —*

> "(Even) the king of demons is able to make a naraka in which to deal with wicked men; why should not I, who am the lord of men, make a naraka in which to deal with wicked men?" He forthwith asked his ministers who could make for him a naraka and preside over the punishment of wicked people in it. They replied that it was only a man of extreme wickedness who could make it; and the king thereupon sent officers to seek everywhere for (such) a bad man; and they saw by the side of a pond a man tall and strong, with a black countenance, yellow hair, and green eyes, hooking up the fish with his feet, while he called to him birds and beasts, and, when they came, then shot and killed them, so that not one escaped. Having got this man, they took him to the king, who secretly charged him, "You must make a square enclosure with high walls. Plant in it all kinds of flowers and fruits; make good ponds in it for bathing; make it grand and imposing in every way, so that men shall look to it with thirsting desire; make its gates strong and sure; and when any one enters, instantly seize him and punish him as a sinner, not allowing him to get out. Even if I should enter, punish me as a sinner in the same way, and do not let me go. I now appoint you master of that naraka."

Soon after this a bhikṣhu, pursuing his regular course of begging his food, entered the gate (of the place). When the lictors of the naraka saw him, they were about to subject him to their tortures; but he, frightened, begged them to allow him a moment in which to eat his midday meal. Immediately after, there came in another man, whom they thrust into a mortar and pounded till a red froth overflowed. As the bhikṣhu looked on, there came to him the thought of the impermanence, the painful suffering and insanity of this body, and how it is but as a bubble and as foam; and instantly he attained to Arhatship. Immediately after, the lictors seized him, and threw him into a cauldron of boiling water. There was a look of joyful satisfaction, however, in the bhikṣhu's countenance. The fire was

> *extinguished, and the water became cold. In the middle (of the caldron) there rose up a lotus flower, with the bhikshu seated on it. The lictors at once went and reported to the king that there was a marvellous occurrence in the naraka, and wished him to go and see it; but the king said, 'I formerly made such an agreement that now I dare not go (to the place).' The lictors said, "This is not a small matter. Your majesty ought to go quickly. Let your former agreement be altered." The king thereupon followed them, and entered (the naraka), when the bhikshu preached the Law to him, and he believed, and was made free. Forthwith he demolished the naraka, and repented of all the evil which he had formerly done. From this time he believed in and honoured the Three Precious Ones, and constantly went to a patra tree, repenting under it, with self-reproach, of his errors, and accepting the eight rules of abstinence."* [8]

We should note that in this account the conversion of Aśoka to Buddhism has nothing to do with the Kalinga war.

6.3 Devānāmpriya Priyadarśī from Inscriptions

To get an idea of what Devānāmpriya Priyadarśī was like, let's go through his 14 major rock edicts as given in the "Inscriptions of Aśoka" by Hultzsch [9].

"First Rock Edict: Shahbazgarhi

> *This rescript on morality has been caused to be written by king Devānāmpriya. Here no living being must be killed and sacrificed. And also no festival meetings must be held. For king Devānāmpriya Priyadarśin sees much evil in festival meetings. But there are also some festival meetings which are considered meritorious by king Devānāmpriya Priyadarśin. Formerly in the kitchen of king Devānāmpriya Priyadarśin many hundred thousands of animals were killed daily for the sake of curry. But now, when this rescript on morality is written, then only three animals are being killed*

(daily), (viz.) two-2-peacocks (and) 1 deer, (but) even this deer not regularly. Even these three animals shall not be killed in future.

Second Rock Edict: Shahbazgarhi

Everywhere in the dominions of Devānāmpriya Priyadarśin, and (of those) who (are his) borderers, such as the Choḍas, the Pāṇdyas, the Satiyaputra, the Keraḍaputra, Tāmrapaṃi, the Yona king named Antiyoka, and the other kings who are the neighbours of this Antiyoka, everywhere two-2-(kinds of) medical treatment were established by king Devānāmpriya Priyadarśin, (viz.) medical treatment for men and medical treatment for cattle. Wherever there were no herbs beneficial to men and beneficial to cattle, everywhere they were caused to be imported and planted. And wells were caused to be dug for the use of cattle and men.

Third Rock Edict: Shahbazgarhi

King Devānāmpriya Priyadarśin speaks (thus). (When I had been) anointed twelve years, [the following] was ordered [by me].

Everywhere in my dominions the Yuktas, the Rajuka, (and) the Prādeśika shall set out on a complete tour (throughout their charges) every five-5-years for this very purpose, (viz.) for the following instruction in morality as well as for other business. Meritorious is obedience to mother and father. [Liberality] to friends, acquaintances, and relatives, to Brāhmaṇas and Śramaṇas [is meritorious]. Abstention from killing animals is meritorious. Moderation in expenditure (and) moderation in possessions are meritorious. The councils (of Mahāmātras) also shall order the Yuktas to register (these rules) both with (the addition of) reasons and according to the letter.

Fourth Rock Edict: Shahbazgarhi

In times past, for many hundreds of years, there had ever been promoted the killing of animals and the hurting of living beings, discourtesy to relatives, (and) discourtesy to Śramaṇas and Brāhmaṇas. But now, in consequence of the practice of morality on the part of king Devānāmpriya Priyadarśin, the sound of drums has become the sound of morality, showing the people representations of aerial chariots, elephants, masses of light, and other divine figures. Such as they had not existed before for many hundreds of years, thus there are now promoted, through the instruction in morality on the part of king Devānāmpriya Priyadarśin, abstention from killing animals, abstention from hurting living beings, courtesy to relatives, courtesy to Brāhmaṇas and Śramaṇas, obedience to mother and father, (and) to the aged. In this and many other ways is the practice of morality promoted. And this practice of morality will be ever promoted by king Devānāmpriya Priyadarśin. And also the sons, grandsons, and great-grandsons of king Devānāmpriya Priyadarśin will ever promote this practice of morality until the aeon (of destruction of the world), (and) will instruct (people) in morality, abiding by morality and by good conduct. For this is the best work, viz. instruction in morality. And the practice of morality also is not (possible) for (a person) devoid of good conduct. Therefore promotion and not neglect of this object is meritorious. For the following purpose has this been written, (viz. in order that) they should devote themselves to the promotion of this practice, and that they should not approve the neglect (of it). (This) conception (jñāna) was caused to be written here by king Devānāmpriya Priyadarśin (when he had been) anointed twelve years.

Fifth Rock Edict: Shahbazgarhi

King Devānāmpriya Priyadarśin speaks thus. It is difficult to perform virtuous deeds. He who starts performing virtuous deeds accomplishes something difficult. Now, by me many virtuous deeds have been performed. Therefore (among) my sons and grandsons, and (among) my descendants who shall come after them until the aeon (of destruction of the world), those who will conform to this (duty) will perform good deeds. But he who will neglect even one (portion) of this (duty) will perform evil deeds. For sin is easily committed. Now, in times past (officers) called Mahāmātras of morality did not exist before. But Mahāmātras of morality were appointed by me (when I had been) anointed thirteen years. These are occupied with all sects in establishing morality, in promoting morality, and for the welfare and happiness of those who are devoted to morality (even) among the Yonas, Kamboyas, and Gandhāras, among the Raṭhikas, among the Pitinikas, and whatever (other) western borderers (of mine there are). They are occupied with servants and masters, with Brāhmaṇas and Ibhyas, with the destitute, (and) with the aged, for the welfare and happiness of those who are devoted to morality, (and) in freeing (them) from desire (for worldly life). They are occupied in supporting prisoners (with money), in causing (their) fetters to be taken off, (and) in setting (them) free, (if) one has children, or is bewitched, or aged, respectively. They are occupied everywhere, here and in all the outlying towns, in the harems of my brothers, of (my) sisters, and (of) whatever other relatives (of mine there are). These Mahāmātras of morality are occupied everywhere in my dominions with those who are devoted to morality, (in order to ascertain) whether one is eager for morality, or established in morality, or furnished with gifts. For the following purpose has this rescript on morality been written, (viz. that) it may be of long duration, and (that) my descendants may conform to it.

Sixth Rock Edict: Shahbazgarhi

King Devānāmpriya Priyadarśin speaks thus. In times past neither the disposal of affairs nor the submission of reports at any time did exist before. But I have made the following (arrangement). Reporters have to report to me the affairs of the people at any time (and) anywhere, while I am eating, in the harem, in the inner apartment, at the cowpen, in the palanquin, (and) in the park. And everywhere I am disposing of the affairs of the people. And also, if in the council (of Mahāmātras) a dispute arises, or an amendment is moved, in connexion with any donation or proclamation which I am ordering verbally, or (in connexion with) an emergent matter which has been delegated to the Mahāmātras, it must be reported to me immediately, anywhere, (and) at any time. Thus I have ordered. For I am never content in exerting myself and in dispatching business. For I consider it my duty (to promote) the welfare of all men. And the root of that (consists) in this, (viz.) exertion and the dispatch of business. For no duty is more important than (promoting) the welfare of all men. And whatever effort I am making, (is made) in order that I may discharge the debt (which I owe) to living beings, (that) I may make them happy in this (world), and (that) they may attain heaven in the other (world). For the following purpose has this [rescript on] morality been written, (viz. that) it may be of long duration, and (that) my sons (and) grandsons may display the same zeal for the welfare of all men. But it is indeed difficult to accomplish this without great zeal.

Seventh Rock Edict: Shahbazgarhi

King Devānāmpriya Priyadarśin desires (that) all sects may reside everywhere. For all these desire self-control and purity of mind. But men possess various desires (and) various passions. They will fulfil either the whole or only a portion (of their duties). But even one who (practises) great liberality, (but) does not possess self-control, purity of mind, gratitude, (and) firm devotion, is very mean.

Eighth Rock Edict: Shahbazgarhi

In times past the Devānāmpriyas used to set out on so-called pleasure-tours. On these (tours) hunting and other such pleasures were (enjoyed). But when king Devānāmpriya Priyadarśin had been anointed ten years, he went out to Saṃbodhi. Therefore tours of morality (were undertaken) here. On these (tours) the following takes place, (viz.) visiting Śramaṇas and Brāhmaṇas (and) making gifts (to them), visiting the aged and supporting (them) with gold, visiting the people of the country, instructing (them) in morality, and questioning (them) about morality, as suitable for this (occasion). This second period (of the reign) of king Devānāmpriya Priyadarśin becomes a pleasure in a higher degree.

Ninth Rock Edict: Shahbazgarhi

King Devānāmpriya Priyadarśin speaks thus. Men are practising various ceremonies during illness, at the marriage of a son or a daughter, at the birth of a child, (and) when setting out on a journey; on these and other such (occasions) men are practising many ceremonies. But in such (cases) women are practising many and various offensive and useless ceremonies. Now, ceremonies should certainly be practised. But these (ceremonies) bear little fruit indeed. But the following bears much fruit indeed, viz. the practice of morality. Herein the following (are comprised), (viz.) proper courtesy to slaves and servants, reverence to elders, gentleness to animals, (and) liberality to Śramaṇas and Brāhmaṇas; these and other (virtues) are called the practice of morality. Therefore a father, or a son, or a brother, or a master, (or) a friend or an acquaintance, (or) even a (mere) neighbour ought to say: 'This is meritorious. This practice should be observed until the (desired) object is attained, (thinking): After it is actually attained, I shall observe this again'. For such ceremonies are of doubtful (effect). One may attain his object (by them), but he may not (do so). And they (bear fruit) in this world only. But that practice of morality is not restricted to time. But if one does not attain (by it) his object in this (world), then endless merit is produced in the other (world). But if one attains (by it) his object (in this world), the gain of both (results) arises from it; (viz.) the (desired) object (is attained) in this (world), and endless merit is produced in the other (world) by that practice of morality.

Tenth Rock Edict: Kalsi

King Devānāmpriya Priyadarśin does not think that either glory or fame conveys much advantage, except whatever glory or fame he desires (on account of his aim) that in the present time, and in the future, men may (be induced) by him to practise obedience to morality, or that they may conform to the duties of morality. On this (account) king Devānāmpriya Priyadarśin is desiring glory and fame. And whatever effort king Devānāmpriya Priyadarśin is making, all that (is) only for the sake of (merit) in the other (world), (and) in order that all (men) may run little danger. But the danger is this, viz. demerit. But it is indeed difficult either for a lowly person or for a high one to accomplish this without great zeal (and without) laying aside every (other aim). But among these (two) it is indeed (more) difficult to accomplish just for a high (person).

Eleventh Rock Edict: Shahbazgarhi

King Devānāmpriya Priyadarśin speaks thus. There is no such gift as the gift of morality, acquaintance through morality, the distribution of morality, (and) kinship through morality. Herein the following (are comprised), (viz.) proper courtesy to slaves and servants, obedience to mother and father, liberality to friends, acquaintances, and relatives, to Śramaṇas and Brāhmaṇas, (and) abstention from killing animals. Concerning this a father, or a son, or a brother, or a master, (or) a friend or an acquaintance, (or) even a (mere) neighbour, ought to say: 'This is meritorious. This ought to be done'. If one is acting thus, he attains (happiness in) this world, and endless merit is produced in the other (world) by that gift of morality.

Twelfth Rock Edict: Shahbazgarhi

King Devānāmpriya Priyadarśin is honouring all sects: (both) ascetics and householders, with gifts and with honours of various kinds. But Devānāmpriya does not value either gifts or honours so (highly) as (this), (viz.) that a promotion of the essentials of all sects should take place. But the promotion of the essentials (is possible) in many ways. But its root is this, viz. guarding (one's) speech, (i.e.) that neither praising one's own sect nor blaming other sects should take place on improper occasions, or (that) it should be moderate in every case. But other sects ought to be duly honoured in every way. If one is acting thus, he is promoting his own sect and is benefiting other sects as well. If one is acting otherwise than thus, he is hurting his own sect and wronging other sects. For whosoever praises his own sect (or) blames other sects,-all (this) out of pure devotion to his own sect, (i.e.) with the view of glorifying his own sect,-if he is acting thus, he rather injures his own sect very severely. Therefore self-control alone is meritorious, (i. e.) that they should both hear and obey each other's morals. For this is the desire of Devānāmpriya, (viz.) that all sects should be both full of learning and pure in doctrine. And those who are attached to their respective (sects), ought to be spoken to (as follows). Devānāmpriya does not value either gifts or honours so (highly) as (this), (viz.) that a promotion of the essentials of all sects should take place. And many (officers) are occupied for this purpose, (viz.) the Mahāmātras of morality, the Mahāmātras controlling women, the inspectors of cowpens, and other classes (of officials). And this is the fruit of it, (viz.) that the promotion of one's own sect takes place, and the glorification of morality.

Thirteenth Rock Edict: Shahbazgarhi

When king Devānāmpriya Priyadarśin had been anointed eight years, (the country of) the Kaliṅgas was conquered by (him). One hundred and fifty thousand in number were the men who were deported thence, one hundred thousand in number were these who were slain there, and many times as many those who died. After that, now that (the country of) the Kaliṅgas has been taken, Devānāmpriya (is devoted) to a zealous study of morality, to the love of morality, and to the instruction (of people) in morality. This is the repentance of Devānāmpriya on account of his conquest of (the country of) the Kaliṅgas. For, this is considered very painful and deplorable by Devānāmpriya, that, while one is conquering an unconquered (country), slaughter, death, and deportation of people (are taking place) there. But the following is considered even more deplorable than this by Devānāmpriya. (To) the Brāhmaṇas or Śramaṇas, or other sects or householders, who are living there, (and) among whom the following are practised: obedience to those who receive high pay, obedience to mother and father, obedience to elders, proper courtesy to friends, acquaintances, companions, and relatives, to slaves and servants, (and) firm devotion, -to these then happen injury or slaughter or deportation of (their) beloved ones. Or, if there are then incurring misfortune the friends, acquaintances, companions, and relatives of those whose affection (for the latter) is undiminished, although they are (themselves) well provided for, this (misfortune) as well becomes an injury to those (persons) themselves. This is shared by all men and is considered deplorable by Devānāmpriya. And there is no (place where men) are not indeed attached to some sect. Therefore even the hundredth part or the thousandth part of all those people who were slain, who died, and who were deported at that time in Kaliṅga, (would) now be considered very deplorable by Devānāmpriya. And Devānāmpriya thinks that even (to one) who should wrong (him), what can be forgiven is to be forgiven. And even (the inhabitants of) the forests which are (included) in the dominions of Devānāmpriya, even those he pacifies (and) converts. And they are told of the power (to punish them) which Devānāmpriya (possesses) in spite of (his) repentance, in order that they may be ashamed (of their crimes) and may not be killed. For Devānāmpriya desires towards all beings abstention from hurting, self-control, (and) impartiality in (case of) violence. And this conquest is considered the principal one by Devānāmpriya, viz. the conquest by morality.

And this (conquest) has been won repeatedly by Devānāmpriya both here and among all (his) borderers, even as far as at (the distance of) six hundred yojanas, where the Yona king named Antiyoka (is ruling), and beyond this Antiyoka, (where) four-4-kings (are ruling), (viz. the king) named Turamaya, (the king) named Antikini, (the king) named Maka, (and the king) named Alikasudara, (and) towards the south, (where) the Choḍas and Pāṇḍyas (are ruling), as far as Tāmrapaṃī. Likewise here in the king's territory, among the Yonas and Kamboyas, among the Nabhakas and Nabhitis, among the Bhojas and Pitinikas, among the Andhras and Palidas,-everywhere (people) are conforming to Devānāmpriya's instruction in morality.

Even those to whom the envoys of Devānāmpriya do not go, having heard of the duties of morality, the ordinances, (and) the instruction in morality of Devānāmpriya, are conforming to morality and will conform to (it). This conquest, which has been won by this everywhere,-a conquest (won) everywhere (and) repeatedly,-causes the feeling of satisfaction. Satisfaction has been obtained (by me) at the conquest by morality. But this satisfaction is indeed of little (consequence). Devānāmpriya thinks that only the fruits in the other (world) are of great (value). And for the following purpose has this rescript on morality been written, (viz.) in order that the sons (and) great-grandsons (who) may be (born) to me, should not think that a fresh conquest ought to be made, (that), if a conquest does please them, they should take pleasure in mercy and light punishments, and (that) they should regard the conquest by morality as the only (true) conquest. This (conquest bears fruit) in this world (and) in the other world. And let there be (to them) pleasure in the abandonment of all (other aims), which is pleasure in morality. For this (bears fruit) in this world (and) in the other world.

Fourteenth Rock Edict: Shahbazgarhi

These rescripts on morality have been caused to be written by king Devānāmpriya Priyadarśin either in an abridged (form) or at full length. For the whole was not suitable everywhere. For (my) dominions are wide, and much has been written, and I shall cause still (more) to be written. But (some) of this has been stated again and again because of the charm of certain topics, (and) in order that men should act accordingly. But some of this may have been written incompletely, either on account of the locality, or because (my) motive was not liked, or by the fault of the writer."

I will comment on the edicts in the section that now follows.

6.4 Aśoka Maurya vs. Devānāmpriya Priyadarśī

It is time now to compare what we know of Aśoka Maurya from literature with what we know of Devānāmpriya Priyadarśī from his inscriptions, and figure out whether both these personalities are one and the same as presented in modern history books.

6.4.1 The Conquest of Kaliṅga

According to Rock edict 13, the conquest of Kaliṅga and the remorse from the ravages of war were the most important events in the life of Devānāmpriya Priyadarśī, but these events find no mention in the literature about Aśoka Maurya. The Kaliṅga war was the turning point in the life of Devānāmpriya Priyadarśī, when he decided to change his ways, preach non-violence, and start following the teachings of Buddhism. How can literary sources be silent about the Kaliṅga war, if Aśoka Maurya was Devānāmpriya

Priyadarśī? Here is what Prof. Basham, author of "The Wonder that was India" says:

> *"One would expect the compilers of this cycle of legends to have recorded the story of the Kalinga war and Aśoka's repentance and embroidered it with many supernatural incidents. Instead, they ignored it." [10]*

6.4.2 The Conversion to Buddhism

According to Rock edict 13, the Kaliṅga war was the main factor behind the conversion of Devānāmpriya Priyadarśī to Buddhism. However, according to the Mahayana tradition, Aśoka converted to Buddhism due to the patience shown by a Buddhist monk under torture, and according to the Theravada tradition, he was converted by a seven year old monk [11]. We have read about the conversion of Aśoka by a Buddhist monk under torture in the travel details of Fa-Hien in Section 6.2. Obviously, Devānāmpriya Priyadarśī was not the same person as Aśoka Maurya.

6.4.3 Third Buddhist Council

According to literary sources, the Third Buddhist Council was held under the patronage of Aśoka Maurya, but there is no mention of it in the edicts of Devānāmpriya Priyadarśī. The absence is very glaring, as Devānāmpriya Priyadarśī describes matters of far less significance in his edicts about what he has done to promote Dharma.

6.4.4 The Family

Aśoka had sent his son Mahendra and daughter Sanghamitrā to Sri Lanka to spread Buddhism. There is no mention of them in the edicts of Devānāmpriya Priyadarśī. From the inscription on the Allahabad Pillar, we know that Kāruwākī was the wife of Devānāmpriya Priyadarśī and Tīvara was their son. However, both

Kāruwākī and Tīvara are not mentioned in literary sources about Aśoka Maurya.

In the fifth rock edict, Devānāmpriya Priyadarśī mentions his brothers and sisters, while according to Dipavansa and Mahavansa, Aśoka had killed all his 99 stepbrothers save his own brother Tissa. We have no mention of the killing of step brothers in any of the inscriptions. Also, there is no mention of Tissa in any of his inscriptions. We find it strange that there is not a single person that is common to both literary sources about Aśoka Maurya and the inscriptions of Devānāmpriya Priyadarśī.

6.4.5 Vegetarianism

When we read in Kalhaṇa's Rājataraṅgiṇī (1.101-102) that Aśoka was a Jain before he converted to Buddhism, we would be naturally skeptical if not shocked. Jainas are known to be non-violent and propagated non-violence. If that was so, why would Aśoka convert from Jainism to Buddhism? However, this is also corroborated from Jain accounts. Chandragupta Maurya, grandfather of Aśoka Maurya, was a Jain, who had spent the later days of his life serving the Jain saint Bhadrabāhu. Aśoka's grandson Samprati is considered the "Constantine of Jainism". He did for Jainism what Aśoka did for Buddhism. So if Aśoka's grandfather was a devout Jain, and his grandson was a devout Jain, it is natural to assume that Aśoka Maurya was born a Jain. As Jains and Buddhists are both vegetarians, Aśoka was a vegetarian before and after conversion to Buddhism. However, Devānāmpriya Priyadarśī says in his edicts that before his conversion hundreds of thousands of animals were killed daily in the royal kitchen. This would be incompatible or contradictory information if Aśoka was always a vegetarian, first as a Jain and then as a Buddhist.

6.4.6 Tolerance

Aśoka, who is considered an apostle of non-violence, was not so tolerant even after his conversion to Buddhism. Mukhopadhyaya translates a story from Aśokāvadāna about Aśoka as follows [12]:

> *"A follower of the Nirgrantha (Mahāvīra) painted a picture, showing Buddha prostrating himself at the feet of Nirgrantha. Aśoka ordered all the Ājīvikas of Pundravardhana (North Bengal) to be killed. In one day, eighteen thousand Ājīvikas lost their lives. A similar kind of incident took place in the town of Pāṭaliputra. A man who painted such a picture was burnt alive with his family. It was announced that whoever would bring the king the head of a Nirgrantha would be rewarded with a Dinara (a gold coin). As a result of this, thousands of Nirgranthas lost their lives."*

John S. Strong also narrates this story in his translation of Aśokāvadāna, so there is no doubt about this story being a part of Aśokāvadāna [13]. This is in contrast to the character of Devānāmpriya Priyadarśī, who had completely given up violence after accepting Buddhism.

These facts should create doubts in our minds about Devānāmpriya Priyadarśī and Aśoka Maurya being the same person. If the Devānāmpriya Priyadarśī of the inscriptions does not match the Aśoka Maurya known from literature, then we must look beyond Aśoka Maurya and search for the real Devānāmpriya Priyadarśī.

Let us take that search up now.

6.5 Face to face with Devānāmpriya Priyadarśī

If Devānāmpriya Priyadarśī was not Aśoka Maurya, and if Aśoka Maurya was a Jain before becoming a Buddhist, we need to search for the real Devānāmpriya Priyadarśī. Based on the fact that the inscriptions of Devānāmpriya Priyadarśī have been found over a wide area covering most of India as well as Bangladesh, Pakistan and Afghanistan, it is obvious that we are not looking for some petty ruler, but someone well-known to historians, though not as Devānāmpriya Priyadarśī. This narrows down the potential number of kings who could be Devānāmpriya Priyadarśī.

I began by scouring books on ancient Indian history in search of Devānāmpriya Priyadarśī. Fortunately, I came across a series of books in Hindi by an accomplished historian, Śrīrāma Goyala, at the Robarts Library, University of Toronto. It was when I was reading his "Gupta Sāmrājya kā Itihāsa" [14], which translates to "A History of Gupta Empire" that I discovered the correct identity of Devānāmpriya Priyadarśī. In his discussion on the coins of Kumāragupta I, Śrīrāma Goyala describes fourteen types of coins issued by Kumāragupta I [15]. The last type of coin is named "Apratigha", which means "not to be vanquished". It has an image in the front of three people. There is a woman on the right side and there is a man on the left side. In the middle, there is an emperor dressed as a monk ("bhikṣu") and it seems that the man and woman are trying to stop him from becoming a monk. It immediately struck me that it was Kumāragupta I who was the emperor I was searching for. Here is an emperor whose kingdom could have covered the area where the inscriptions of Devānāmpriya Priyadarśī have been discovered from. There is also proof of him becoming a monk, from what we can see in the image imprinted on his coins. It was a tantalizing possibility that needed further investigation.

The next step was to check how long Kumāragupta I ruled since the rock edicts of Devānāmpriya Priyadarśī mention that some of the edicts were inscribed during the twenty-sixth year of his reign. According to history books, Kumāragupta I ruled for 40 years: so, there would be no problem in identifying him as Devānāmpriya Priyadarśī. Further conviction was offered after I read the Junagarh rock inscription of Skandagupta in which he describes his father as having attained the friendship of gods. Finally, I was convinced beyond doubt about the identity of Kumāragupta I as

Devānāmpriya Priyadarśī when I read Śrīrāma Goyala's interpretation of a verse from Viṣṇupurāṇa to mean that Kumāragupta I added Kaliṅga and Māhiṣaka to Gupta territory [16].

Let us now examine the evidence in support of Kumāragupta I being the Devānāmpriya Priyadarśī of inscriptions.

6.5.1 The Kaliṅga War

The following verse from Viṣṇupurāṇa describes the expansion of the Imperial Gupta Empire [16]:

"Kośala Oḍratāmraliptān Samudrataṭa Purīm cha Rakṣito Rakṣyati|
Kaliṅgam Māhiṣakam Mahendraḥ Bhūmau Guham Bhokṣyanti||"

Śrīrāma Goyala explains the meaning of this verse as follows:

> *"(Deva) Rakṣita will expand his domain to Kośala, Oḍra, Tāmralipti and Purī near ocean. Kaliṅga and Māhiṣaka will be under Mahendra. All this land will be ruled by Guha."*

Here "rakṣita" stands for Gupta as the meaning of both words is "protected". Kośala was an ancient kingdom located in present day Uttar Pradesh. Oḍra was an ancient kingdom located in the northern part of present day Orissa/Odisha. Tāmralipti was a famous port represented by current day Tamluk in Midnapore district of West Bengal. Purī is the current day Purī district in Odisha. Kaliṅga was an ancient kingdom south of Oḍra located in present day Odisha and northern parts of Andhra Pradesh and Telangana. Māhiṣaka was an ancient kingdom located in present day Karnataka.

Since all the places mentioned in this verse are in eastern and southern part of India except Kośala, it is my contention that Kośala in this verse stands for Dakṣina Kośala, which was an ancient kingdom located in present day Chhatisgarh and Western Odisha. Also, Samudrataṭa, which means ocean shore, may represent the ancient region of Samataṭa located in Southeastern Bengal. Samataṭa is mentioned as one of the regions under the rule of Samudragupta in his Allahabad pillar inscription. Mahendra stands for Kumāragupta I Mahendrāditya. Guha stands for Skandagupta, as Guha and Skanda are synonyms. Śrīrāma Goyala presumes "Deva" before Rakṣita or Gupta to imply that Devagupta, which is supposedly another name for Chandragupta II, will expand his domain to Kośala, Oḍra, Tāmralipti and Purī near the ocean. In my opinion, this assumption is not warranted as this important verse gives the following information:

> *Gupta (Chandragupta II) will protect the territories of (South) Kośala, Oḍra, Tāmralipti, Samataṭa and Purī (which are already part of Gupta empire). Kumāragupta I will expand it further to include Kaliṅga and Māhiṣaka. Skandagupta will enjoy ruling all this land.*

Here we have emphatic proof that Kaliṅga was not a part of Gupta Empire ruled by Chandragupta II, and was conquered by Kumāragupta I. This is the war that changed Kumāragupta I, and he accepted Buddhism soon after.

Let us compare this to Aśoka Maurya for whom we have no independent information that he had to fight a war to incorporate Kaliṅga to his empire. In fact, the evidence points to the opposite. Aśoka should have inherited Kaliṅga as it was part of the Nanda Empire, which was taken over by his grandfather Chandragupta in a coup. He did not have to wage war to capture Kaliṅga. To avoid this situation, modern historians have made up a story about Kaliṅga gaining independence from the Mauryan Empire before the coronation of Aśoka. There is absolutely no evidence to this effect. In fact, there is evidence to the contrary. Chāṇakya is supposed to have served three kings -- Chandragupta, Bindusāra and Aśoka -- according to the medieval text Ārya-Manjuśrī-Mūlakalpa. Noted historian K.P. Jayaswal writes [17]:

> *"The historical detail about him, which is important, is that he lived in three reigns, triṇi rājyani. Chandragupta seems to have died comparatively young. ... Bindusara reigned for 25 years ... Chāṇakya must have come down to the opening years of Aśoka, to be the mantrin in three reigns. He would have thus maintained the unity of the Maurya policy for over 50 years in his person."*

Thus, it would have been very unlikely for Kaliṅga to secede under the watch of Chāṇakya, the man who overthrew the mighty Nanda Empire to avenge Dhana Nanda's insult that he was an ugly-looking man.

6.5.2 The Junagadh Rock Inscription

Skandagupta, son of Kumāragupta I, says the following in line 4 of the Junagadh rock inscription [18]:

"Pitari sura-sakhitvam prāptvaty ātma- śaktyā"

Since this sentence has never been interpreted the way I am going to interpret now, the meaning of each word in this sentence is provided below:

Pitari = father, sura = Gods, sakhitvam = friendship, prāptvaty = obtain, ātma = self and śaktyā = from power

Thus the sentence means that the father obtained the friendship of the Gods by his own power. Historians have taken it to mean that Kumāragupta I had passed away when this inscription was recorded, as it is customary in India to say that a person has become dear to God when he or she has passed away. However, we need to then ask how could Kumāragupta I do it with his own power? Did he commit suicide? We don't have any record of that, and if he did commit suicide, why would his son Skandagupta be proudly announcing it? This is nothing to be proud of. What this sentence means is that Kumāragupta I had obtained the friendship of the Gods by his own power while he was still alive. At least that is what his son Skandagupta was made to believe. Why would he not believe so anyway? His father Kumāragupta I had declared himself as "Beloved of the Gods" in inscriptions all over the vast empire. He was just paraphrasing the word "Devānāmpriya" meaning "Beloved of the Gods" as "Friend of the Gods". Thus, here we have an acknowledgment from Skandagupta that his father Kumāragupta I had adopted the name "Beloved of the Gods".

6.5.3 Man of many Names

I will now provide proof that Kumāragupta I was known as a man with many names as he called himself by other names such as "Devānāmpriya" and "Priyadarśī". Ārya-Mañjuśrī-Mūlakalpa is a text in Sanskrit language written by a Buddhist around 800 CE. It was translated into English by noted historian K. P. Jayaswal. This text gives the following information about the Imperial Guptas [19]:

> *"Listen about the Medieval and Madhyadesa kings (madhyakāle, madhyamā) who will be in a long period emperors (nṛpendra) and who will be confident and will be followers of via media" (in religious policy, madhyadharmiṇaḥ):*
> *(1) Samudra, the king,*
> *(2) Vikrama, of good fame (kīrttitāḥ), 'who is sung'.*
> *(3) Mahendra, an excellent king and a leader (nṛpavaro Mukhya).*
> *(4) S-initialled (Skanda) after Ma. (i.e., Mahendra).*
> *His name (will be) Devarāja; he will have several names (vividhākhya); he will be the best, wise and religious king in that low age."*

In this excerpt we find that the first king is Samudragupta; the second king is Chandragupta II called by the first part of his title Vikramāditya; the third king is Kumāragupta I identified by the first part of his title Mahendrāditya; and, the fourth king is Skandagupta identified by his initial "S". I would like to draw your attention to the description of the king called Devarāja above, who was supposed to have several names. Jayaswal has identified him with Skandagupta as follows [20]:

> *"After Ma. (i.e., Mahendra) the succession of S. (i.e., Skanda) is specifically noted, and V. Smith is confirmed here. He bore the name of his grandfather (Devarāja) and had a variety of names (virudas).*
>
> *The most important thing about this king is the highest praise reserved for him:*
>
> *the best (śreshṭha),*
> *a wise (buddhimān)*
> *and justice-loving (dharma-vatsala)*
> *king in that low age (yugādhame)'.*
>
> *This estimate of his character is noteworthy. He was in the opinion of the Indian historian, the greatest of the great Gupta sovereigns. I may be permitted to add here that this has been my own humble opinion. He was the greatest of the Gupta kings. He was the only hero in Asia and Europe who could defeat the Huns at their rise. This he did at an early age which is evident from the Bhitari pillar inscription. His wise administration is attested to by Chakrapālita's Junagarh inscription."*

I would like to differ. The author of Ārya-Mañjuśrī-Mūlakalpa is not talking about Skandagupta, but his father Kumāragupta I. the author says "S-initialled (Skanda) after Ma" and then goes on to say "His name (will be) Devarāja". He continues with the description of M-initialled where the previous sentence ends. It is also clear from the description where he has been called Devarāja, i.e., king of the Gods, which is Indra. Jayaswal says that Skandagupta bore the name of his grandfather (Devarāja), and had a variety of names (virudas). There is absolutely no evidence that Skandagupta bore the name of Devarāja after his grandfather. In the case of Kumāragupta I it is obvious as his title is Mahendrāditya and he has been called Mahendra by the author of Ārya-Mañjuśrī-Mūlakalpa as quoted above. However, Mahendra (Mahā + Indra) is simply "the great Indra" or Indra himself. Thus it is Kumāragupta I who has been called Devarāja, and therefore he had a variety of names. This view is also supported by the personal belief of the author of Ārya-Mañjuśrī-Mūlakalpa, who as a Buddhist could not believe that anyone could be a good person without being a Buddhist. This viewpoint becomes obvious by even a cursory reading of the text Ārya-Mañjuśrī-Mūlakalpa. Jayaswal has made the following comments regarding the description of Chandragupta, Bindusāra, and Chāṇakya in this text [21].

> *"Only these two names are given under the dynasty of Chandragupta. Aśoka the Great is already misplaced above. The succession of Bindusāra as a minor is noteworthy, and also his character sketch which was wanting up to this time. He was not a Buddhist. An explanation was therefore due. How could a king be successful without having been a Buddhist? He had as a child raised a toy stūpa of dust. This every Indian child does even to-day. The common form of their play is to raise a mound of dust.*
>
> *Chandragupta was not a Buddhist. His military career was punished by his illness and poisonous boils.*
>
> *Chāṇakya has come in for a lot of abuse and deliverance into hell. In his Arthaśāstra he has penalised embracing monkish life without providing for one's family and without state permission. He was hard on Buddhists otherwise. The Buddhist history must have its revenge by assigning such a statesman at least to a long career in hell on paper."*

Why would the author of Ārya-Mañjuśrī-Mūlakalpa say good things about Skandagupta, if he is so full of hatred towards non-Buddhists? Skandagupta is not known to have done anything special for Buddhists. The conclusion is obvious. All the encomiums are for Kumāragupta I as he had not only become a Buddhist, but dedicated his life to spreading Buddhism as proven from his inscriptions as Devānāmpriya Priyadarśī. The most important contribution of Kumāragupta I was the establishment of Nālandā University.

6.5.4 Confusion and more Confusion

When Kumāragupta I started on his mission to be the grand patron of Buddhism, he had the example of Aśoka Maurya to emulate. It seems that historian Kalhaṇa was confused between these two benefactors of Buddhism. According to Kalhaṇa, Aśoka had a son named Jalauka [22]. According to the Tumain inscription, Kumāragupta I was protecting the earth as if she was his wife. This idea is very unique, and we find that Kalhaṇa used the same description for a king he calls Pratāpāditya whose son is named Jalaukas [23]. It stands to reason that Kalhaṇa was confused between Aśoka Maurya and Kumāragupta I, and he was not sure whose son Jalauka was. Therefore, he wrote that Aśoka's son was Jalauka and Kumāragupta's son was Jalaukas.

Kalhaṇa was not the only person before the modern historians to be confused about Aśoka Maurya. Here is another case of confusion, this time by a Chinese pilgrim, as described by Barua [24].

> *"The hymn of praise composed in honour of the Trikāya and set up at Bodhgayā by a later Chinese pilgrim, named Chiang Hsia Pias, wrongly describes the great temple of Bodhgayā as a memorable erection of Aśoka".*

6.5.5 The Prayāga (Allahabad) pillar

There are several sets of inscriptions on the Allahabad pillar currently located in the Allahabad Fort including inscriptions by Devānāmpriya Priyadarśī, his queen, and most importantly Samudragupta. There is also an inscription by Moghul Emperor Jahangir on this pillar. Here, my intention is to focus on the inscription by Samudragupta, who according to the modern chronology, was posterior to Devānāmpriya Priyadarśī by over six centuries. Samudragupta was the greatest conqueror known to Indian history. His eulogy inscribed on this pillar gives the details of his conquests and the expanse of his empire. As Samudragupta was posterior to Aśoka Maurya according to modern history, this pillar is known as Aśokan pillar, and Samudragupta's eulogy is supposed to have been inscribed on it later. My contention is to challenge the prevailing wisdom and propose that it was Samudragupta who erected the pillar, and it was Devānāmpriya Priyadarśī's inscriptions that were inscribed later on this pillar. Samudragupta was known for the re-establishment of traditional Vedic/Hindu way of life. There is simply no reason for Samudragupta to have his eulogy inscribed on an existing pillar with inscriptions by a Buddhist king as his zeal for military conquests did not match the pacifist ideology of Devānāmpriya Priyadarśī. Thapar, wondering why Samudragupta chose to write his eulogy on the Aśokan pillar, says that extolling military conquest was contradictory to Aśoka's opposition to violence and if Samudragupta wanted to denigrate Aśoka, it would have been more effective on a separate and equally imposing pillar [25].

It is inconceivable that such a great monarch as Samudragupta, whose generosity was legendary, would use Aśoka Maurya's pillar for writing his eulogy. Samudragupta was so generous as to give away one hundred thousand cows (line 25). He called himself the God of Wealth Kubera (line 26). He further said that his officials were busy returning the wealth of defeated kings everyday (line 26). Why would such a monarch not be able to afford a pillar of his own and choose a pillar erected by Budhist monarch Aśoka Maurya to write his eulogy? Why would he describe an existing pillar as a symbol of his glory? In the lines 29-30 of his inscription on the Allahabad pillar, Samudragupta says with pride that this pillar is looking towards the heaven as the declaration of his glory [26]. On the other hand, Devānāmpriya Priyadarśī, identified as

Kumāragupta I by me, would have been more than happy to add his inscriptions on Samudragupta's pillar as his proud grandson. Since this evidence is so critically damaging to the accepted chronology, let's go into the details of the various aspects of the Allahabad pillar as described by Alexander Cunningham [27].

> *"The well known Allahabad pillar is a single shaft of polished sandstone 35 feet in length, with a lower diameter of 2 feet 11 inches, and an upper diameter of 2 feet 2 inches. The capital of the column was no doubt of the usual bell shape of Aśoka's other pillars, but of this there is now no trace. The circular abacus, however, still remains with its graceful scroll of alternate lotus and honeysuckle, resting on a beaded astragalus of Greek origin. This was once surmounted by the statue of a lion; but the lion must have disappeared many centuries ago, as when the pillar was re-erected by Jahāngir in A.D. 1605, it was crowned by a globe, surmounted by a cone, as described and sketched by Padre Tieffenthaler in the middle of the next century. It then stood in the middle of the fort.*
>
> *The great inscription of Aśoka, containing the same series of six edicts which are found on the four pillars, is engraved in continuous lines around the column. The letters are uniform in size, and are very neatly and deeply engraved. But a great portion of the third and fourth edicts, comprising seven lines, has been ruthlessly destroyed by the cutting of vainglorious inscription of Jehāngir, recording the names of his ancestors. Two lines of the fifth edict are nearly intact, but nearly the whole of the remainder has been lost by the peeling off of the surface of the stone. The sixth edict is complete with the exception of about half a line.*
>
> *Immediately below the Aśoka edicts comes the long and well-known inscription of Samudra Gupta. The upper portion of this inscription is confined between a crack in the stone on its left, and two short Aśoka inscriptions on its right. The lower one of these, consisting of five lines, was translated by Prinsep, and as it refers to Aśoka's queens, I propose to name it "the Queen's edict." But the upper*

inscription, consisting of four lines, was discovered by myself, and as it is addressed to the rulers of Koshambi, I propose to name it "the Koshambi edict." All that remains of these Aśoka edicts is given in Plate XXII of the Pillar inscriptions.

Of middle age inscriptions there is no trace, but the mass of short records in rudely cut modern Nāgari covers quite as much space as the two inscriptions of Aśoka and Samudra. Above the Aśoka edicts there is a mass of this modern scribbling equal in size to the Samudra Gupta inscription. But besides this, the whole of the Aśoka inscription is interlined with the same rubbish, which is continued below on all sides of the two shorter edicts, one of which has been half obliterated by the modern letters.

Regarding these minor inscriptions, James Prinsep remarks that "it is a singular fact that the periods at which the pillar has been overthrown can thus be determined with nearly as much certainty from this desultory writing as can be epochs of its being re-erected from the more formal inscriptions recording the latter event. Thus that it was overthrown some time after its first erection by the great Aśoka in the middle of the third century before Christ, is proved by the longitudinal or random insertion of several names in a character intermediate between No. 1 and No. 2, in which the m, b &c., retain the old form."

Of one of these names he remarks, - 'Now it would have been exceedingly difficult, if not impossible, to have cut the name No. 10 up and down at right angles to the other writing, while the pillar was erect, to say nothing of the place being out of reach, unless a scaffold was erected on purpose, which would hardly be the case, since the object of an ambitious visitor would be defeated by placing his name out of sight and in an unreadable position. The pillar was erected as Samudra Gupta's arm, and there it probably remained until overthrown again by the idol-breaking zeal of the Musalmans; for we find no writings on it of the Pala or Sarnath type (i.e. of the tenth century), but a quantity appears with plain legible dates from the Samvat year 1420, or A.D. 1363, down to 1660 odd, and it is remarkable that these occupy one side of the shaft, or that which was uppermost when the pillar was in a prostrate position. A few detached and ill-executed Nāgari names with Samvat dates of 1800 odd show that ever since it was laid on the ground again by General Garstin, the passion for recording visits of piety or curiosity has been at work.'

I have gone through the mass of modern scribbling in the hope of finding something that might throw further light on the history of the pillar, and I have not been altogether disappointed. I have found seven dates ranging from Samvat 1297 to 1398, or from A.D. 1240 to 1341; five ranging from Samvat 1464 to 1495, or A.D. 1407 to 1438; twelve ranging from Samvat 1501 to 1584, or A.D. 1444 to 1527; three ranging from Samvat 1632 to 1640, or A.D. 1575 to 1583; and three of Samvat 1864, or A.D. 1807. These dates, combined with the total absence of any mediaeval Nāgari inscriptions, are sufficient to show that the pillar was standing out of the reach of pilgrim's scribbling from the time of the Guptas until that of the early Musalman kings of Delhi. There are then twelve dated inscriptions coming down to near the death of Muhammad Tughlak. There is not a single record of the time of Firoz Tughlak which leads me to suspect that he may have re-erected this pillar with its globe and cone, like those of the Zarin-Minar, or Golden Pillar, at Delhi. But if he did set it up, it must have been thrown down again during the troubled times of his immediate successors, as the dates begin again in A.D. 1407 and 1408. It was next set up by Jahangir in A.H. 1014, or A.D. 1605, to be pulled down by General Kyd in A.D. 1798. It was once more scribbled upon in A.D. 1807, and finally in 1838 it was set up as it stands at present.

From the address of Aśoka to the rulers of Kosāmbi, in the newly discovered edict, it seems probable that this pillar may have been originally erected in that city, and afterwards removed to Prayāg or Allahabad. But if so, the removal was not made by Jahāngir, as I have found amongst the modern Nāgari records a short inscription of the famous Birbar, the companion and favourite of Akbar. The words of the short record are as follows:

Samvat 1632, Sāke 1493, Mārgabadi panchami.

1. *Somwār Gangādās sut Maharaja Birba(r) Sri.*
2. *Tirth Rāj Prayāg ke jātrā Saphal lekhitam*

"In the Samvat year 1632, Sāke 1493, in Marga, the 5th of the waning moon, on Monday, Gangādās's son Maharaja Birba(r) made the auspicious pilgrimage to Tirth Rāj Prayāg. Saphal scripsit."

The Samvat date is equivalent to A.D. 1575, and as the building of the fort of Allahabad was finished in A.H. 982 = A.D. 1572, it is probable that Birbar took advantage during one of his attendances on Akbar to pay a visit to the meeting of the waters of the Gangā and Yamuna under the holy tree of Prayāga. But whatever may have been the occasion of Birbar's visit, its record is sufficient to prove that the pillar was then lying on the ground at Prayāga. If then, it was originally erected at Kosāmbi, it seems highly probable that it must have been brought to Prayāga by Firoz Tughlak, whose removal of Siwālik and Mirat pillars to Delhi gives countenance to this suggestion. The silence of the Chinese pilgrim Hwen Thsang is also in favour of my suggestion that the present Allahabad pillar was originally set up at Kosāmbi."

So it is the opinion of modern historians that the pillar was originally erected at Kauśāmbi as there is an inscription of Devānāmpriya Priyadarśī addressed to his officials at Kauśāmbi. Kauśāmbi is about 55 km west of Allahabad. The pillar fell down and was erected again by Samudragupta at Kauśāmbi itself. It was brought from Kauśāmbi and erected at Allahabad by Firoz Shah Tughlaq. It was brought down by the successors of Firoz Shah Tughlak and finally erected again in its present position by the British. In contrast to this convoluted theory, I offer this proposition: the pillar was erected by Samudragupta for the purpose of writing his eulogy at Allahabad. His grandson Devānāmpriya Priyadarśī added his inscriptions on this pillar. It was brought down by invaders in the thirteenth century CE and erected in its present position by British. As the pillar was already standing, Devānāmpriya Priyadarśī took the opportunity to address his officials using this pillar. The officials from Kauśāmbi might have been visiting Prayāga as part of official business. There is no evidence that this pillar was ever at Kauśāmbi. Devānāmpriya Priyadarśī already had a pillar at Kauśāmbi. Why would he not use that pillar for this inscription? There is no reason for Firoz Shah Tughlaq to have brought this pillar from Kauśāmbi to Allahabad. He could have taken it to Delhi like other pillars, if he had anything to do with it. Also, there is no evidence that pillar was lying on the ground during the time of Samudragupta. His inscriptions were inscribed before the erection of the pillar. It would have been very difficult to inscribe parts of his inscription as pointed by Prinsep above, if the pillar was already standing on the ground.

The pillar was erected at Allahabad as it was one of the capitals of the Imperial Guptas. The possibility of Prayāga being one of the capitals of the Imperial Guptas has been discussed in detail in Chapter 5. The realization that Devānāmpriya Priyadarśī wrote his inscriptions on an existing pillar erected by Samudragupta has far reaching implications, and with this single piece of evidence the whole edifice of modern Indian chronology falls like a pack of cards.

Now, let me present another piece of evidence in support of my theory.

6.5.6 Mauryan and Gupta Brāhmī

Inscriptions of Samudragupta and Devānāmpriya Priyadarśī are both written in Brāhmī. According to modern historians, Aśoka Maurya was Devānāmpriya Priyadarśī. So, the inscriptions of Samudragupta are supposed to be written in Gupta Brāhmī and the inscriptions of Devānāmpriya Priyadarśī are supposed to be written in Mauryan Brāhmī. Suppose that Devānāmpriya Priyadarśī was Kumaragupta I as I have proposed, then both the inscriptions would be written in Gupta Brāhmī. As Kumaragupta I was the grandson of Samudragupta, there should not really be much of a difference between the scripts used by Samudragupta and Devānāmpriya Priyadarśī. Here is the proof of my proposition [28]:

> *"Thus, while legends of Aśoka persisted and were transmitted in Buddhist texts and royal lineages were recorded in the Puranas, detailed knowledge of the historical Aśoka and the empire he ruled appears to have been lost relatively rapidly. And by the late fourth century CE, Brahmi script had disappeared from usage. When the Chinese pilgrim Hsuan-tsang visited India in the early seventh century, he recognized the large sculpted columns he saw at several sites as associated with the legendary ruler. But neither he nor earlier pilgrims such as Fa-hien were able to read the Aśokan inscriptions on them."*

When Fa-hien came to India in the late fourth century CE, as per modern historians Chandragupta II was ruling. Fa-hien makes no mention of him, which is surprising. What is more surprising is that he could not find anybody who knew Brāhmī. The Imperial Guptas were still using Brāhmī, which may have been somewhat different than Mauryan Brāhmī if we believe modern chronology, but certainly it could not have been so different that nobody could read the inscriptions of Devānāmpriya Priyadarśī. This is consistent with the Imperial Guptas being removed by several centuries in time from Fa-hien so that Brāhmī had no longer been in use for several centuries when Fa-hien visited India.

6.6 Tying the Loose Ends

It is time now to tie the loose ends. If Kumaragupta I was the real Devānāmpriya Priyadarśī of major rock edicts and pillar edicts, then how do we explain the minor rock edicts associating

"Devānāmpriya" with Aśoka? The name Aśoka appears in a few minor rocks edicts as "Devānām Piya Aśoka" at Maski in Raichur district, Karnataka, as "Rājā Aśoko Devānāmpiya" at Udegolam in Bellary district, Karnataka and as "Devānāmpiya Piyadasi Aśoka Rājā" at Gujarra near Jhansi, Madhya Pradesh [29]. In addition, versions of minor rock edicts I and II containing the name Aśoka have been found at Nittur in Tumkur district in the state of Karnataka. In order to find a way out of this situation, which looks like a dead end, we will need to understand the meaning of each of these terms and their usages in South Asian literature.

6.6.1 The Meaning of Devānāmpriya

Devānāmpriya means "beloved of the Gods". We find this title being used by many kings. When Prinsep was translating the inscriptions of Priyadarśī, he identified him first with Devānāmpiya Tissa of Ceylon as shown in the following two excerpts:

> *"… I trust this point has been set at rest, and that it has been satisfactorily proved that the several pillars of Delhi, Allahabad, Mattiah and Radhia were erected under the orders of king Devanampiya Piyadasi of Ceylon, about three hundred years before the Christian era." [30]*

> *"It is a well known fact that Aśoka's name does not occur in his inscriptions, but that these purport to emanate from a king who gives his formal title in various Prakrit forms of which the Sanskrit would be Devanampriyah Priyadarshi raja. The great decipherer of the old Brahmi alphabet, James Prinsep, at first ascribed Aśoka's edicts to Devanampiya Tissa of Ceylon. The discovery of the Nagarjuni Hill cave inscriptions of Dashalatha Devanampiya, whom he at once identified with Dasharatha, the grandson of the Maurya king Aśoka, and the fact that Turnour had found Piyadassi or Piyadassana used as surname of Aśoka in the*

Dipavansha, induced Prinsep to abandon his original view, and to identify Devanampriya Priyadarshin with Aśoka himself." [31]

We can see from above that Devānāmpriya was used as a title by King Daśaratha as well. Apart from the inscriptions, this title has been used for other personalities in literature. King Ajātaśatru has been called "Devanuppiya" in "Aupapatika Sūtra". Patañjali, commenting on Pāṇini's Aṣṭādhyāyī 2.4.56, has used this title for a common grammarian. In Indian literature Kātyāyana (probably third century BCE), in his commentary on Panini's Aṣṭādhyāyī 6.3.21, has said that fools are called Devānāmpriya. It is indeed possible that such uses came into effect due to the Brahmins' dislike of the Buddhists. Also worth noting is the Hindi word "Buddhu" meaning "fool" with its origin in the word "Buddha". Possibly, it was in response to Buddhists making fun of Brahmins by calling them "Brahmabandhu". The point to note is that the title Devānāmpriya was a common title, not a personal name, and could have been used by any king who liked this title.

6.6.2 The Meaning of Priyadarśī

Priyadarśī or Priyadarśana can have two meanings: one who looks handsome, or one who looks with friendliness. Priyadarśī was an adjective that has been used for several kings. In the Rāmāyaṇa, Rāma has been called Priyadarśī once. In the play Mudrārākṣasa, Chandragupta Maurya, grandfather of Aśoka Maurya, has been called Priyadarśī. Gautamīputra Sātakarṇi has been called Priyadarśana in the Nasika inscription. Thus, by itself the use of a title like Priyadarśī does not make the identification unique, as this title could have been used by other kings as well. There is nothing unique about it.

6.6.3 The Meaning of Aśoka

The word Aśoka is made by joining "A" meaning "no/not" with "Śoka" meaning "sorrow". Thus Aśoka means one who has no sorrow. This raises the possibility that Aśoka may also be used as a title just like Devānāmpriya and Priyadarśī. It need not be a personal name. In Sanskrit literature, the term Priyadarśana has been used as a constant epithet of the Aśoka tree, so much so that Priyadarśana became another name for the Aśoka tree. [32]

There are therefore two possible explanations for the inscriptions containing the word Aśoka: the first possibility is that the minor rock edicts belong to Aśoka Maurya, but the major rock edicts containing the names of five Greek kings belong to Kumāragupta I. The second possibility is that all edicts under consideration belong to Kumāragupta I, and the word Aśoka has been used as a title just as the words Devānāmpriya and Priyadarśī. Kumāragupta I had the example of Aśoka Maurya to follow, and possibly he was being urged by Buddhist monks to match what Aśoka Maurya had done for the spread of Buddhism. As Aśoka means one who is beyond the feeling of suffering, and the central philosophy of Buddhism is the elimination of suffering, becoming Aśoka is the aim of every Buddhist. Thus, when Kumāragupta I considered himself to have attained this state, and considered himself to have matched Aśoka Maurya in his endeavours to spread Buddhism, Kumāragupta I might have adopted the title Aśoka. This viewpoint is tenable in the light of the fact that Aśoka Maurya's last name "Maurya" does not appear in the inscriptions. Following this line of thought further, if Kumāragupta I had indeed adopted the title Aśoka, then it would certainly have caused confusion among earlier writers just as it did to European scholars. Two examples of this confusion have been given in Section 6.5.4 above. All that we need to conclude the case is to make the closing arguments about the five Greek kings mentioned in the thirteenth rock edict.

6.6.4 And then there were five

The five Greek kings mentioned in the Rock Edict XIII are: Antiyoka, Turamaya, Antikini, Maka, and Alikasudara. Modern historians have identified them with Antiochus II Theos (261-246 BCE) of Syria and Western Asia, Ptolemy II Philadelphus (285-247 BCE) of Egypt, Antigonus Gonatas (278-239 BCE) of Macedonia, Magas (300-258 or 250 BCE) of Cyrene and Alexander (275-255 BCE) of Epirus or Alexander (252-247 BCE) of Corinth respectively [33].

Based on this information, historians have been able to pinpoint the date of coronation of Aśoka to within a couple of years [34]:

> *"The latest date at which these kings were reigning together is 258, the earliest 261; and if we could be certain that Aśoka was kept informed of what happened in the West, we might therefore fix the twelfth year of his reign between these two years; and hence the date of his coronation between 270 and 273 B.C."*

Modern historians have identified all the Greek kings mentioned by Devānāmpriya Priyadarśī and narrowed down to two years, when the Rock Edict 13 was inscribed. It seems that modern historians have the case so foolproof that it is impossible to crack it. However, there has to be something wrong with this picture in the light of what we have discussed in this book so far. Let's take a closer look at the relevant text of Rock Edict 13 [35]:

> *"Antiyoke nāma Yona Rāja paran cha tena*
> *Antiyokena chatura rājāne Turamaye nāma*
> *Antikini nāma Maka nāma Alikasandare nāma"*

The text has following meaning: "The Greek king named Antiyoka and beyond that king Antiyoka, four kings, named Turamaya, named Antikini, named Maka, named Alikasandara". It is obvious that Devānāmpriya Priyadarśī had close interaction with King Antiyoka or Antiochus and he probably had just heard about the other four Greek kings. When Prinsep first identified King Antiyoka, he had identified him with Antiochus III and not Antiochus II as done by current historians. Why is this of so much importance? Our answer lies in the following quote [36]:

"It is too well known to need more than a formal repetition here that two of the Rock Edicts of Aśoka mention as his contemporaries a number of kings of the West, the foremost of which is a certain Antiochus. ...

> "Now this conquest, viz. the conquest by (preaching) Buddhism, is considered the highest one by the Beloved of the Gods. And even this conquest has been won by the Beloved of the Gods here and in all the borderlands as far as six hundred yojanas where (lives) Antiochus, king of the Yavanas (Westerners), and beyond this Antiochus four (4) kings, Ptolemy by name, Antigonus by name, Magas by name, Alexander by name."

Less illuminating is the passage in the second Rock Edict ...

> "Antiochus, king of the Yavanas, and those other kings who are the vassals of this Antiochus ..."

Now, who is this Antiochus, king of the Yavanas? To this question various replies have been given, and it may not be out of the way shortly to review them here. Prinsep, JASB. vii, 156 sqq., when first interpreting these inscriptions, suggested that we have here a mention of Antiochus III who, during the earlier part of his reign, rightly earned the surname of "the Great". This suggestion was only a natural one; for Antiochus III is the one of all the Seleucids bearing that famous name of whose dealings with the Indians we are aware. ... Prinsep, when making the above-mentioned suggestion, was not yet aware of the contents of Rock Edict XIII. A little later on, having deciphered also this edict, he abandoned his former idea and instead of Antiochus III suggested the first or second king of that name: "of whom the former may have the preference from his close family connection with both Ptolemy and Magas, which would readily give him the power of promising free communication between India and Egypt.

Wilson, JRAS. (O.S.) xii, 244 ff., arrived at the queer conclusion that the five kings mentioned in Rock Edict XIII were not contemporaries. To quote his own words (p. 246): "Under this view I should refer Alexander to Alexander the Great, Antigonus to his successor, Magas to the son-in-law of Ptolemy Philadelphus, Ptolemy to either or all of the four first princes of Egypt, and Antiochus to the only one of the number who we know from classical authors did visit India ... Antiochus the Great." Wilson afterwards tells us that it seems highly improbable that Aśoka should still have been alive in the year 205 B.C., upon which he fixed as being that of Antiochus's Indian campaign; this, consequently, would exclude Antiochus III. And he likewise finds it utterly incredible that the Yavana king could be Antiochus II- this chiefly because of the Bactrian and Parthian rebellions occurring during his reign. As, however, Wilson did not admit the identity of Aśoka and Piyadasi, all his arguments must needs end in a non liquet. ...

The chief interest is, however, concentrated upon the identity of Antiochus. As we have already mentioned above, modern scholarly opinion seems to have fairly unanimously fixed upon the second monarch of that name. Personally I am inclined gravely to doubt this conclusion as I shall explain presently. As an introductory remark I shall only emphasize my opinion that, whoever be this Antiochus, there is not the slightest reason for assuming that the man mentioned in Rock Edicts XIII and II would not be the same person. Antiochus II, surnamed probably by the grateful Milesians Theos, "the god," was the younger son of Antiochus I Soter, whom he succeeded between October, 262, and April, 261 B.C. at the age of about twenty-four. He died rather suddenly in 246 B.C. (or possibly late in 247, cf. Cambridge Ancient Hist., vii, 716) at the age of scarcely more than forty. He, like at least one of his successors, seems to have been a, special favourite with the scandalmongers of the period. Phylarchus, most foul-mouthed perhaps amongst Greek historians, tells us shocking stories about his drunken bouts and his inclination towards young men of somewhat dubious accomplishments. Some or even most of this may be true;

but we still may do well in taking note of the warning uttered by one of the best modern authorities on the history of the Seleucids.

What interests us in this connection is, however, not so much the character of Antiochus II as the main events of his reign. He undoubtedly inherited from his father a war with Egypt, which came to an end only during his very last years, and an unbroken series of troubles with the petty despots and quarrelsome city-states of Asia Minor. As far as the very scanty evidence goes, Antiochus II spent the whole of his reign in the last-named country and in Syria; and there is certainly no evidence whatsoever for his having ever proceeded to the east of the Mesopotamian rivers to visit the outlying provinces of his vast and loosely-knitted empire. Furthermore, we have the direct evidence of the historians, above all that of Justin, the epitomator Pompei Trogi, that during the reign of Antiochus II the most important provinces of the east rebelled, an event which must have entirely cut off the connections between Mesopotamia and the borderlands of India until these were again, for a very short period of time, restored by Antiochus the Great."

So we find that that Antiochus II could not possibly have been the Antiochus mentioned in the major rock edicts. There was no way Antiochus II could have been in touch with Devānāmpriya Priyadarśī. But this is the Antiochus that modern historians have identified as the contemporary of Devānāmpriya Priyadarśī based on the identification of the other four Greek kings mentioned by Devānāmpriya Priyadarśī.

On the other hand, identification of Antiyoka with Antiochus III fits perfectly with the identification of Kumāragupta I with Devānāmpriya Priyadarśī. Starting with Chandragupta I as a contemporary of Alexander the Great, the reign of Kumāragupta I will overlap with the reign of Antiochus III about whom we have definite information that he arrived at the border of India. If Antiochus III the Great was the contemporary of Devānāmpriya Priyadarśī, how do we account for the other four kings, all of whom are certainly not ruling during the revised time period of Kumāragupta's rule (213-173 BCE)? It seems that we are stuck again. We need not worry, however, as the answer has been provided by Professor H.H. Wilson, Director of the Royal Asiatic Society, in 1850 CE itself as follows [37]:

> *"That they were so applied is rendered doubtful by chronological difficulties, of which it is not easy to dispose: Piyadasi appears to have lived, either at the same time with, or subsequent to, Antiochus. Could this have been the case if he was Aśoka? For the determination of this question, we must investigate the date at which the two princes flourished, so far as the materials are available will permit.*
>
> *The first point to be adjusted is, which Antiochus is referred to. There are several of the names amongst the kings of the Seleucidan dynasty, whose sway commencing in Syria, extended at various times, in the early periods of their history, through Persia to the confines of India. Of these, the two first, Antiochus Soter and Antiochus Theos, were too much taken up with concurrences in Greece and in the west of Asia, to maintain any intimate connexion with India, and it is not until the time of Antiochus the Great, the fifth Seleucid monarch, that we have any positive indication of an intercourse between India and Syria. It is recorded of this prince that he invaded India, and formed an alliance with its sovereign, named by Greek writers, Sophagasenas, in the first member of which it requires the etymological courage of a Wilford to discover Aśoka. The late Augustus Schlegel conjectured the Greek name to represent the Sanskrit, Saubhagya Sena, he whose army is attended by prosperity; but we have no such prince in Hindu tradition, and it could scarcely have been a synonym of Aśoka, the literal sense of which is, he who has no sorrow. Neither is Sophagasenas more like Piyadasi, and so far therefore we derive no assistance as to the identification of Antiochus. Still, with reference to the facts, and to the allusion to his victorious progress, which Tablet XIII*

seems to contain, we can scarcely doubt that he was the person intended, and that the Antiochus of the inscription is Antiochus the Great, who ascended the throne, B.C. 223, and was killed, B.C. 187. The date of his eastern expedition is from B.C. 212 to B.C. 205.

There is, however an obvious difficulty in the way of the identification from the names of the princes which are found in connexion with that of Antiochus, and which the thirteenth Tablet appears to recapitulate as those of contemporary princes, subjugated, if the conjectural interpretation be correct, by Antiochus. With respect to one of them, Ptolemy, this is allowable, for Antiochus the Great engaged in war with Ptolemy Philopator, the fourth king of Egypt, with various success, and concluded peace with him before he undertook his expedition to Bactria and India. He therefore was contemporary with Antiochus the Great. It is, however, to be recollected that Ptolemy Philopator was preceded by three other princes of the same name, Ptolemy Soter, Ptolemy Philadelphus, and Ptolemy Euergetes, extending through a period of rather more than a century, or from B.C. 323 to B.C. 221. These princes were frequently engaged in hostilities with the Seleucidian kings of Syria, and we cannot therefore positively determine which of them is referred to in the inscription. The long continuance of the same name, however, among the kings of Egypt, as it was retained until the Roman conquest, no doubt made it familiar throughout the East, and we need not be surprised to find it at Kapur di Giri or Girnar.

The same circumstances will not account for the insertion of the name of Mako, probably Magas, for although there was such a prince, he was far removed from India, and of no particular celebrity. Magas was made ruler of Cyrene by his father-in-law, Ptolemy Soter, the first Greek king of Egypt, about B.C. 308. He had a long reign of fifty years, to B.C. 258. He was not therefore contemporary with Antiochus the Great, dying thirty five years before that prince's accession. He was connected with Antiochus

Soter, having married his daughter, and entered into an alliance with him against Ptolemy Philadelphus, and this association with the names of Antiochus and Ptolemy, generally but not accurately known, may have led to his being enumerated with the two other princes of the same designation, Ptolemy Philopater, and Antiochus the Great. There was a Magas also, the brother of Philopater, but he is of no historical note, and was put to death by his brother in the beginning of his reign. The allusion is therefore, no doubt to the Magas the Cyrene.

It is impossible to explain the juxtaposition of the other two names, Antigonus and Alexander, upon any principle of chronological computation, although we can easily comprehend how the names were familiarly known. That of Alexander the Great must of course have left a durable impression, but he is antecedent to any of his generals who made themselves kings after his death. It is very unlikely that his son Alexander, who was not born till after his death, and from the age of three years was brought up in Macedonia, where he was murdered when only twelve years old, should be the person intended, and a greater probability would attach to an Alexander who was Satrap of Persia in the beginning of the reign of Antiochus the Great, and rebelled against him. He was defeated and killed, B.C. 223. So far therefore we have an Alexander contemporary with Antiochus, if that be thought essential; but it seems that here as in the case of Magas, the concurrence of names is no evidence of synchronism, and arises from the name being familiarly known without any exact knowledge of the persons by whom they were borne.

Such seems to be the case also with respect to Antigonus. The most celebrated of the name, Alexander's general who succeeded to the sovereignty of Phyrgia and Lycia, extended his authority to the East by the defeat and death of Eumenes, and his name may thus have become known in India, although the scene of his victories over his rival was somewhat remote from the frontier, or in Persia and Media. The latter portions of his career were

> *confined to Asia Minor and Greece, and he was killed B.C. 301. He was contemporary with the first Ptolemy but not with Antiochus, having been killed twenty years before the accession of Antiochus Soter, We have another Antigonus, the Grandson of the preceding, who was contemporary with Antiochus Soter, but his life was spent in Macedonia and Greece, and it is not likely therefore that anything should have been known of him in India. It can only be the first Antigonus whose designation reached an Indian prince, and the mention of him in conjunction with Ptolemy, Antiochus, Magas, and Alexander, shows clearly that the chronology of the inscription was utterly at fault if it intended to assign a contemporary existence to princes who were scattered through, at least, an interval of a century.*
>
> *We must look, therefore, not to dates, but to the notoriety of the names, and the probability of their having become known in India, for the identification of the persons intended. Under this view, I should refer Alexander to Alexander the Great, Antigonus to his successor, Magas to the son-in-law of Ptolemy Philadelphus, Ptolemy to either or all of the four first princes of Egypt, and Antiochus to the only one of the number, who we know from classical record did visit India, who from the purport of the inscriptions we may infer was known there personally, Antiochus the Great. In this case we obtain for the date of the inscription some period subsequent to B.C. 205, at which it seems very unlikely that Aśoka was living."*

The views of Prof. Wilson, which have been neglected by current historians in favor of the accepted chronology, need to be taken seriously in the light of many revelations made in this book. We need to understand that all the Greek kings mentioned by Devānāmpriya Priyadarśī were not his contemporaries. If someone asks me here in Canada -- "Where are you from?" and I say, "I am from the land of Swāmī Vivekānanda", does it make me the contemporary of Swāmī Vivekānanda? If we look at this carefully, how could Devānāmpriya Priyadarśī be so current about far away kings of distant lands? How can the period of the writing of Rock Edict 13 be specified within a narrow range of time of two years? Kings could change by the time information reached Devānāmpriya Priyadarśī. In fact, Devānāmpriya Priyadarśī accepts in Rock Edict II that he did not know the names of the four kings who reigned beyond the land of Antiochus by saying "Yona king named Antiyoka, and the other kings who are the neighbours of this Antiyoka." Thus the correct purport of Rock Edict XIII is "where the Yona king named Antiyoka (is ruling) and beyond this Antiyoka, **(the land of)** four kings (the king) named Turamaya, (the king) named Antikini, (the king) named Maka, (and the king) named Alikasudara". Thus while Antiochus was definitely his contemporary, the other four kings -- Ptolemy, Antigonus, Magas and Alexander -- were either his contemporaries or before his time. With this argument, I believe I have satisfactorily answered all objections to the identification of Kumaragupta I with Devānāmpriya Priyadarśī.

It follows from my reasoning that the extent of the Imperial Gupta Empire was much larger than the extent of the Maurya Empire, which is drawn by enclosing the areas where the inscriptions of Devānāmpriya Priyadarśī have been found. In fact, what is shown as the extent of the Maurya Empire in textbooks is the extent of the Imperial Gupta Empire. As Devānāmpriya Priyadarśī was Kumaragupta I and not Aśoka Maurya, the actual extent of the Maurya Empire will be hard to demarcate.

The identification of Sandrokottos with Chandragupta I and Devānāmpriya Priyadarśī with Kumaragupta I, both of the Imperial Gupta Dynasty, should free Indian history from the shackles of the current chronology and provide us the opportunity to reconstruct the history of India as it really happened. This is the task that I take up in the next chapter.

Notes

1. Prinsep (1838a).
2. Prinsep (1838b).
3. Hultzsch (1925): 27-71.
4. Venkatachelam (1953): 8.
5. Vyāsaśiṣya (1988): 181.
6. Sethna (1989): 359.
7. Basham (1982).
8. Legge (1886): 90-92.
9. Hultzsch (1925): 27-71.
10. Basham (1982).
11. Basham (1982).
12. Mukhopadhyaya (1963): xxxvii.
13. Strong (1989): 232.
14. Goyala (1987a).
15. Goyala (1987a): 244-246.
16. Goyala (1987a): 253.
17. Jayaswal (1934): 17.
18. Fleet (1888): 56-65
19. Jayaswal (1934): 33.
20. Jayaswal (1934): 35-36.
21. Jayaswal (1934): 16-17.
22. Rājataraṅgiṇī 1.101-108.
23. Rājataraṅgiṇī 2.5-9.
24. Barua (1968): 2.
25. Thapar (2013): 341.
26. Goyala (1987b): 16-19.
27. Cunningham (1879): 37-39.
28. Alcock (2001): 161.
29. Vassilkov (1997-98).
30. Prinsep (1837).
31. Hultzsch (1914): 943-951.
32. Vassilkov (1997-98).

33. Sethna (1989): 233.
34. Davids (1877): 42.
35. Hultzsch (1925): 86-87.
36. Charpentier (1931).
37. Wilson (1850). Excerpts from pages 244-247.

"We have to overcome with patience what separates us and treasure what brings us closer and unites us."

- Alexander Lukashenko

7. LAND OF THE FEARLESS

"If we consider the political changes and convulsions which have happened in Hindustan since Mahmud's invasion, and the intolerant bigotry of many of his successors, we shall be able to account for the paucity of its national works on history, without being driven to the improbable conclusion that the Hindus were ignorant of an art which has been cultivated in other countries from almost the earliest ages. Is it to be imagined that a nation so highly civilized as the Hindus, amongst whom the exact sciences flourished in perfection, by whom the fine arts, architecture, sculpture, poetry, music, were not only cultivated, but taught and defined by the nicest and most elaborate rules, were totally unacquainted with the simple art of recording the events of their history, the characters of their princes, and the acts of their reigns. Where such traces of mind exist, we can hardly believe that there was a want of competent recorders of events, which synchronical authorities tell us were worthy of commemoration. The cities of Hastinapur and Indraprastha, of Anhilwara and Somanatha, the triumphal columns of Delhi and Chitor, the shrines of Abu and Girnar, the cave temples of Elephanta and Ellora, are so many attestations of the same fact; nor can we imagine that the age in which these works were erected was without an historian. Yet from the Mahabharata or Great War to Alexander's invasion, and from that great event to the era of the Mahmud of Ghazni, scarcely a paragraph of pure native Hindu

history (except as before stated) has hitherto been revealed to the curiosity of western scholars. In the heroic history of Prithiraj, the last of Hindu sovereigns of Delhi, written by his bard Chand, we find notices which authorize the inference that works similar to his own were then extant, relating to the period between Mahmud and Shihabuddin (A.D. 1000-1193), but these have disappeared.

After eight centuries of galling subjection to conquerors totally ignorant of the classical language of the Hindus; after almost every capital city had been repeatedly stormed and sacked by the barbarous, bigoted, and exasperated foes; it is too much to expect that the literature of the country should not have sustained, in common with other important interests, irretrievable losses. My own animadversions upon the defective conditions of the annals of Rajwara have more than once been checked by a very just remark: "when our princes were in exile, driven from hold to hold, and compelled to dwell in the clefts of the mountains, often doubtful whether they would not be forced to abandon the very meal preparing for them, was that a time to think of historical records?" "[1]

These words by Lieutenant Colonel James Tod explain why we don't have proper and necessary records for the reconstruction of ancient Indian history. Tod joined the Bengal Army of East India Company as a 17-year-old and quickly rose through the ranks to become the Political Agent for Rājpūtānā, land of the Rajput kings, who kept fighting for centuries to protect their motherland from the onslaught of barbaric invaders. During his interactions with Rajput kings, Tod developed a deep sympathy for their plight and earned their respect. He was granted access to the still extant records by the Rajput kings. On his return to England, he published his memoirs in three volumes titled "Annals and Antiquities of Rajasthan or the Central and Western Rajput States of India". His work is invaluable in reconstructing the history of Rājpūtānā, the land of the fearless warriors.

Rajputs belonged to the Kṣatriya class (varṇa), one of the four classes the society was divided into by ancient Indians. Kṣatriyas were known for their valor and fearlessness. As long as blood flew in their veins, they would not let an invader set foot on their soil. They were prepared to give their life without hesitation for the sake of their homeland. Kṣatriyas were neither afraid to die nor unwilling to kill to protect their homeland from invaders. One of the most sacred scriptures of Hinduism is the Gītā, which explicitly ordains a Kṣatriya to fight a just war to live with honor instead of avoiding a war to live in ignominy. Here is how Al Biruni explains the teaching of the Gītā:

> *"Further, Vasudeva speaks, inspiring him with courage to fight the enemy: "Dost thou not know, O man with the long arm, that thou art a Kshatriya; that thy race has been created brave, to rush boldly to the charge, to care little for the vicissitudes of time, never to give way whenever their soul has a, foreboding of coining misfortune? For only thereby is the reward to be obtained. If he conquers, he obtains power and good fortune. If he perishes, he obtains paradise and bliss. Besides, thou showest weakness in the presence of the enemy, and seemest melancholy at the prospect of killing this host; but it will be infinitely worse if thy name will spread as that of a timid, cowardly man, that thy reputation among the heroes and the experienced warriors will be gone, that thou wilt be out of their sight, and thy name no longer be remembered among them. I do, not know a worse punishment than such a state. Death is better than to expose thyself to the consequences of ignominy. If, therefore, God has ordered thee to fight, if he has deigned to confer upon thy caste the task of fighting and has created thee for it, carry out his order and perform his will with a determination which is free from any desire, so that thy action be exclusively devoted to him." " [2]*

> *"Such is the condition of the four castes. Arjuna asked about the nature of the four castes and what must be their moral qualities, whereupon Vasudeva answered: "The Brahmana must have an*

> *ample intellect, a quiet heart, truthful speech, much patience; he must be master of his senses, a lover of justice, of evident purity, always directed upon worship, entirely bent upon religion. The Kshatriya must fill the hearts with terror, must be brave and high-minded, must have ready speech and a liberal hand, not minding dangers, only intent upon carrying the great tasks of his calling to a happy end." " [3]*

In spite of the clear message of the Gītā to Kṣatriyas that they be willing and ready to go to war to protect *dharma*, today there is a widely prevalent view among many Hindus that non-violence is the highest *dharma* ("Ahiṃsā paramo dharmaḥ"). Traditionally, this was not applicable to all Hindus, but only to Brāhmaṇas. In the Ādi Parva of the Mahābhārata, it is stated that Ahiṃsā or non-violence was applicable to Brāhmaṇas only due to their nature and was not applicable to Kṣatriyas [4]. In the current context, for example, would it make sense that we ask our military and police forces to practice non-violence?

There are times when violence is to be preferred over non-violence. There is a time for war and there is a time for peace. There will be times when the cost of non-violence will far outweigh the cost of violence. In the face of a brutal enemy non-violence could mean extinction or slavery, and using violence to defend what we hold dear would be the honorable, just and singular way for survival. Non-violence is an ideal and can be justified as an individual pursuit, but would bring unmitigated disaster as the avowed policy of the state. Non-violence is a useless weapon against a ruthless enemy. Professor Hans Bakker has written that though India is known for the principle of non-violence since the days of Mahatma Gandhi, originally non-violence had little or nothing to do with the concept of warfare in Hindu society. He explains the attitude of Hindus in his illuminating article, "The Hindu Religion and War" [5]:

> *"War was endemic in South Asia and seen as the right and duty of the Hindu king. This warfare, however, was regulated by some rules, which were humane in some respects. Battle was sometimes conceived of as a form of ritual, in which the soldiers were the sacrificial victims. This does not imply that Hindu kings went to war for the sake of religion. In this respect Hinduism differed fundamentally from the Semitic religions."*

The concept of Hindus being non-violent is a British creation. They knew that the day Hindus discovered their true identity, the days of British Empire in India would be numbered. It is much easier to rule over non-violent people than an assertive people. The British benefited from propounding the idea of non-violence and Hindus as a non-violent people. Today, a generation of Hindus have been led to believe that India got independence because of non-violent demonstrations. While the non-violent demonstrations led by Mahatma Gandhi did test British leaders they were mostly considered a nuisance in maintaining and protecting British imperialism. If the British had to contend only with non-violent demonstrations, they would still be ruling India.

One has to look at oppressed people around the world to understand what happens to peaceful people relying on non-violent demonstrations. If we live in peace, it is because we have soldiers guarding our borders. If we are known to be non-violent nobody would leave us in peace. India is an ancient land and Hindus have fought battles and wars over millennia. However, because of a complex of forces, Hindus, for nearly two centuries, were made to believe through propaganda that they are a submissive people. Ancient Indians were always in a state of alert, because the barbarians were always at the gates. They made a clear distinction between those who were inside India and those who were outside. Those who were inside were called Ārya or civilized and those who were outside were called Mlechchha or barbarians. Indians rarely attacked the Mlechchhas, but if the Mlechchhas dared to attack India, they were engaged vigorously. Al Biruni talks about the attitude of Indians towards Mlechchhas in these words [6]:

> *"On the whole, there is very little disputing about theological topics among themselves; at the utmost, they fight with words, but they will never stake their soul or body or their property on religious controversy. On the contrary, all their fanaticism is directed against those who do not belong to them—against all foreigners. They call them mlechchha, i.e. impure, and forbid having any connection with them, be it by intermarriage or any other kind of relationship, or by sitting, eating, and drinking with them, because thereby, they think, they would be polluted."*

The defeat of invaders was celebrated across India. Two of the most popular ways of reckoning time in ancient India, Vikrama Saṃvat and Śālivāhana Śaka, were instituted to celebrate the defeat of the Śakas by Vikramāditya and Gautamiputra Śātakarṇi respectively.

It was the job of the Brāhmaṇas to ensure the safety of the state from external as well as internal threats. Brāhmaṇas were known for their purity and selflessness. Their foremost task was the protection of the Vedas, their oldest texts. They succeeded in their mission against all odds, and we are fortunate that due to their unwavering commitment to the protection of the Vedas, we have received the Vedas in the original form they intended. Our task now is to decode and understand the message that our ancestors considered so important to transmit. A section of Brāhmaṇas dedicated their lives to preserve the Vedas. These Brāhmaṇas, called Śrauta Brāhmaṇas because they memorized Śrutis i.e. Vedas, received the highest honour among all Brāhmaṇas. It is because of the sacrifices of the Brāhmaṇas that Indian civilization has endured the ravages of time. Here is how the Chinese traveller Xuan Zang has described the Brāhmaṇas of India [7]:

"The families of India are divided into castes, the Brāhmaṇs particularly (are noted) on account of their purity and nobility. Tradition has so hallowed the name of this tribe that there is no question as to difference of place, but the people generally speak of India as the country of the Brāhmaṇs (Po-lo-men)."

Al Biruni translates a verse by Varāhamihira regarding the exalted state of the Brāhmaṇas as follows [8]:

"One of their scholars, Varahamihira, in a passage where he calls on the people to honour the Brahmans, says: "The Greeks, though impure, must be honoured, since they were trained in sciences, and therein excelled others. What, then, are we to say of a Brahman, if he combines with his purity the height of science?" "

In the Mandasor stone inscription of Kumāragupta I, the following is said about the Brāhmaṇas [9]:

"Like the sky with the brilliant multitudes of planets, it shines with Brāhmans endowed with truth, patience, self-control, tranquillity, religious vows, purity, fortitude, private study, good conduct, refinement, and steadfastness, (and) abounding in learning and penances, and free from the excitement of surprise."

It was because of the life of piety led by the Brāhmaṇas and the fearless valour of the Kṣatriyas that the rest of the society consisting of Vaiśyas and Śūdras could live a life of happiness and prosperity. They could go on with their daily life even when they were working next to a battlefield, as attested by Greeks [10]:

"After these, the second caste consists of the tillers of the soil, who form the most numerous class of the population. They are neither furnished with arms, nor have any military duties to perform, but they cultivate the soil and pay tribute to the kings and the independent cities. In times of civil war the soldiers are not allowed to molest the husbandmen or ravage their lands: hence, while the former are fighting and killing each other as they can, the latter may be seen close at hand tranquilly pursuing their work, perhaps

ploughing, or gathering in their crops, pruning the trees, or reaping the harvest."

When Hindus controlled their destiny, they had rules governing society that were far more humanistic than the contemporary civilizations of the time. While the rest of the world practiced slavery, it was banned in India as attested by the following remarks by the Greeks [11]:

"Of several remarkable customs existing among the Indians, there is one prescribed by their ancient philosophers which one may regard as truly admirable: for the law ordains that no one among them shall, under any circumstances, be a slave, but that, enjoying freedom, they shall respect the equal right to it which all possess: for those, they thought, who have learned neither to domineer over nor to cringe to others will attain the life best adapted for all vicissitudes of lot: for it is but fair and reasonable to institute laws which bind all equally, but allow property to be unevenly distributed."

Ancient Hindu society was not an ideal society nor were the rules completely fair, but only that they were more fair than what prevailed elsewhere.

To subjugate Indian mind, history was used as a weapon of choice. History was distorted to demonize the Brāhmaṇas and debilitate the Hindus by projecting Hindus as a docile people. While that is not the primary thrust of this book, it is important that we wipe the historical mirror clean so that we can see as much of the past as clearly as possible. The first step towards the reconstruction of history is to get the chronology right.

7.1 Magadha after Buddha and Mahāvīra

I have followed the same scientific approach that colonial era historians had followed, which is fixing the sheet anchors of Indian history and then carefully sifting the information to move back and forth from those anchor points. As we have discussed, colonial era historians considered Chandragupta Maurya to be the contemporary of Alexander the Great and Aśoka Maurya to be the contemporary of the Greek kings mentioned in the rock edicts of Devānāmpriya Priyadarśī. We have shown that these sheet anchors need to be changed. We have considered Chandragupta I of the Imperial Gupta Dynasty to be the contemporary of Alexander the Great and Kumāragupta I to be the contemporary of some of the Greek kings mentioned in the rock edicts of Devānāmpriya Priyadarśī. Based on these premises, Table 7.1 presents the chronology that we have worked out for the kings of Magadha from the time of the Buddha and Mahāvīra to the end of the Nanda Dynasty based on regnal years given in the Purāṇas. Our calculations show that the Buddha lived between 1258-1178 BCE and that Mahāvīra lived between 1244-1172 BCE. Detailed justification for these dates is provided in the second volume in this series -- "India after Alexander: The Age of Vikramādityas". The date for Mahāvīra has been calculated based on the commencement of Kṛta/Mālava era in 702 BCE. The date for the Buddha has been calculated based on the information provided in an astronomical text from Nepal. It is only logical that the correct information about the date of the Buddha was preserved near his place of birth. Modern historians have deliberately chosen the records from Sri Lanka, as these records fitted the chronology they had built. There is nothing in the records from Sri Lanka that make them more reliable.

Ārya-Mañjuśrī-Mūlakalpa offers the following information about Vararuchi and Pāṇini [13]:

> *"After him there will be king Nanda at Pushpa-city. ... His minister was a Buddhist Brahmin Vararuchi who was of high soul, kind and good. The king, though true, caused alienation of feeling of the Council of Ministers at Patala City (434-35). The king became very ill, died at 67. His great friend was a Brahmin, Panini by name."*

Table 7.1: The chronology of pre-Maurya kings

Kings	Reign in years	Accepted Chronology [12]	Proposed Chronology
Ajātaśatru	25	492-460 BCE	1185-1160 BCE
Darśaka	25		1160-1135 BCE
Udāyin	33	460-444 BCE	1135-1102 BCE
Udāyin's successors		444-412 BCE	
Nandivardhana	40		1102-1062 BCE
Śiśunāga dynasty		412-344 BCE	
Mahānandin	43		1062-1019 BCE
Mahāpadma Nanda	88	344-323 BCE	1019-919 BCE
Eight Nandas	12	344-323 BCE	1019-919 BCE

Vararuchi is a famous name in Sanskrit literature. Vararuchi was the author of many literary and scientific texts. Pāṇini is well known for the treatise on Sanskrit grammar called Aṣṭādhyāyī. They both adorned the court of King Nanda, who could be Nandivardhana, Mahānandin, Mahāpadma Nanda or any of the eight Nanda kings. Thus we can tentatively fix the time of these two luminaries to tenth century BCE. The chronological framework developed in this book gives us the opportunity to correctly date the scholars from the past.

7.2 Magadha after Nandas

It is well known that the last Nanda king was deposed by Chandragupta Maurya, who established the Maurya dynasty. He became the emperor with the help of Chāṇakya, a Brāhmaṇa who was humiliated by the last Nanda king. The chronology of the kings of Magadha after Nandas can be determined from the regnal years given in the Purāṇas [14]:

"Kauṭilya will anoint Chandragupta as king in the realm. Chandragupta will be king 24 years. Vindusāra will be king 25 years. Aśoka will be king 36 years. His son Kuṇāla will reign 8 years.

Kunāla's son Bandhupālita will enjoy the kingdom 8 years. Their grandson Daśona will reign 7 years. His son Daśaratha will be king 8 years. His son Samprati will reign 9 years. Śāliśūka will be king 13 years. Devadharman will be king 7 years. His son Śatadhanvan will be king 8 years. Bṛhadratha will reign 70 years. These are the 10 Mauryas who will enjoy the earth full 137 years. After them it will go to the Śuṅgas.

Puṣyamitra the commander-in-chief will uproot Bṛhadratha and will rule the kingdom as king 36 years. His son Agnimitra will be king 8 years. Vasujyeṣṭha will be king 7 years. His son Vasumitra will be king 10 years. Then his son Andhraka will reign 2 years. Pulindaka will then reign 3 years. His son Ghoṣa will be king 3 years. Next Vajramitra will be king 9 years. Bhāgavata will be king 32 years. His son Devabhūmi will reign 10 years. These 10 Śuṅga kings will enjoy this earth full 112 years. From them the earth will pass to the Kaṅvas.

The minister Vasudeva, forcibly overthrowing the dissolute king Devabhūmi because of his youth, will become king among the Śuṅgas. He, the Kāṅvāyana, will be king 9 years. His son Bhūmimitra will reign 14 years. His son Nārāyaṅa will reign 12 years. His son Suśarman will reign 10 years. These are remembered as the Śuṅgabhṛtya Kāṅvāyana kings. These 4 Kaṅva Brāhmans will enjoy the earth; for 45 years they will enjoy this earth. They will have the neighbouring kings in subjection and will be righteous. In succession to them the earth will pass to Āndhras."

Based on these regnal years, the proposed chronology of Maurya and post-Maurya kings is shown in Tables 7.2 and 7.3.

Table 7.2: The chronology of Maurya kings

King	Reign in years	Accepted Chronology [15]	Proposed Chronology
Chandragupta	24	324-300 BCE	919-895 BCE
Bindusāra	25	300-273 BCE	895-870 BCE
Aśoka	36	273-236 BCE	870-834 BCE
Kuṇāla	8		834-826 BCE
Bandhupālita	8		826-818 BCE
Daśona	7		818-811 BCE
Daśaratha	8		811-803 BCE
Samprati	9	236-187 BCE	803-794 BCE
Śāliśūka	13		794-781 BCE
Devadharman	7		781-774 BCE
Śatadhanvan	8		774-766 BCE
Bṛhadratha	70		766-696 BCE

Table 7.3: The chronology of post-Maurya kings

King	Reign in years	Accepted Chronology [16]	Proposed Chronology
Puṣyamitra (Śuṅga)	36	188-152 BCE	696-660 BCE
Agnimitra (Śuṅga)	8	152-144 BCE	660-652 BCE
Vasujyeṣṭha (Śuṅga)	7	144-137 BCE	652-645 BCE
Vasumitra (Śuṅga)	10	137-129 BCE	645-635 BCE
Andhraka (Śuṅga)	2	129-127 BCE	635-633 BCE
Pulindaka (Śuṅga)	3	127-124 BCE	633-630 BCE
Ghoṣa (Śuṅga)	3	124-121 BCE	630-627 BCE
Vajramitra (Śuṅga)	9	121-112 BCE	627-618 BCE
Bhāgavata (Śuṅga)	32	112-86 BCE	618-586 BCE
Devabhūmi (Śuṅga)	10	86-76 BCE	586-576 BCE
Vasudeva (Kaṇva)	9	76-67 BCE	576-567 BCE
Bhūmimitra (Kaṇva)	14	67-53 BCE	567-553 BCE
Nārāyaṇa (Kaṇva)	12	53-41 BCE	553-541 BCE
Suśarman (Kaṇva)	10	41-31 BCE	541-531 BCE

We should note here that Aśoka Maurya is called Aśoka the Great in history books, but the greatness attributed to him is because he is identified as Devānāmpriya Priyadarśī. I have shown in the last chapter that this identification is wrong. In the light of this discovery, historians may want to reconsider whether Aśoka Maurya was great or not and whether Kumāragupta I should be given the title of "the Great" as he was the real Devānāmpriya Priyadarśī. Some texts fix the date of ascension of Puṣyamitra at 187 BCE [17-18], in which case the dates from the accepted chronology in Table 7.3 can be moved down by one year to get the corresponding dates.

The last Maurya king, Bṛhadratha, was killed by his army general, Puṣyamitra Śuṅga, who established the Śuṅga dynasty. Kings getting killed when their thrones are usurped is a common feature across the history of the world. As Bṛhadratha was a Buddhist and the person usurping the throne was a Brāhmaṇa, later Buddhists accused him of persecuting Buddhists. However, these accusations have to be taken with a grain of salt as Buddhists were intolerant of other belief systems. They considered the path enunciated by the Buddha as the true path and condemned to hell anyone who they thought was not following the true path.

I have already quoted the example of Chāṇakya having been cursed to spend his time in hell. Here is another example that has been related to Puṣyamitra Śuṅga [19]:

> *"In the Low Age (yugadhame) there will be king, the chief Gomin (Gomimukhya, S.; 'Gomin by name', T.), destroyer of my religion. Having seized the East and the gate of Kashmir, he the fool, the wicked, will destroy monasteries with relics, and kill monks of good conduct. He will die in the North, being killed along with his officers and his animal relations by the fall of a mountain rock. He was destined to a dreadful suffering in hell."*

Noted historian K.P. Jayaswal makes the following comments on this text from ĀryaMañjuśrīMūlaKalpa [20]:

> *"... the king is abused by the expression Gomi-shanda, 'Gomi the bull'. The name is concealed; and the real import of Gomi or Gomin is not clear. But the description shows that the hellish, the animalish king is no other than the Brahmin emperor Pushyamitra. It is definitely stated that Northern India from the Prachi up to the Kashmir valley was under this king."*

I do not believe that Puṣyamitra Śuṅga is being referred to in these verses. There is no similarity between the names Puṣyamitra Śuṅga and Gomi. Who is this Gomi, the persecutor of Buddhists, who deserved a place in hell, according to the author of the Ārya-Mañjuśrī-MūlaKalpa? I believe that these verses refer to Mihirakula. Gomi could be an abbreviation of "Gotra Mihira", i.e. clan of Mihira, which has the same meaning as Mihirakula (Kula or clan of Mihira). Bull, the vehicle of Lord Śiva, may represent that the king was a Śaiva, which Mihirakula was.

The most probable reason for the slaying of Kṣatriya Bṛhadratha by Brāhmaṇa Puṣyamitra Śuṅga seems to be the dereliction of the duty of a king by Bṛhadratha. Under the influence of Buddhism, the kings had abandoned their duty to fight the enemy and protect their subjects. This created a major problem for the Brāhmaṇas, who had sworn to protect the state from internal and external threats. On the religious side, they gave vent to their anger by creating the legends of Paraśurāma, a mythical Brāhmaṇa warrior who annihilated the Kṣatriyas 21 times. On the ground, they picked up the sword themselves to protect the state and called themselves Kṣatropeta Brāhmaṇa, i.e. a Brāhmaṇa who has taken up arms and become a Kṣatriya.

The last Śuṅga king was Devabhūmi, who was overthrown by his minister Vasudeva, who established the Kaṇva dynasty. The last king of the Kaṇva Dynasty was Suśarman, whose reign ended in

531 BCE, according to our calculations. What happened next is uncertain.

7.3 Āndhras

All Purāṇas are unanimous that the Āndhras came to power after overthrowing the last Kaṇva ruler, Suśarman. However, the Āndhras were a South Indian dynasty and there is no independent proof that they ruled from Magadha in North India. Another complication is that the kings listed in the Purāṇas as Āndhra kings call themselves Sātavāhana in their inscriptions. Not only that, they have not referred themselves as Āndhras even once in their inscriptions. Based on the literary evidence in the Purāṇas and inscriptional evidence, modern historians have combined them together as Āndhra-Sātavāhana kings. Indian tradition places the famous Sātavāhana king Gautamīputra Sātakarṇi in first century CE as the Śālivāhana Śaka had been instituted in the memory of him defeating the Śaka kings. Āndhras have been mentioned in the Aitareya Brāhmaṇa, which takes their antiquity to the second millennium BCE, as Brāhmaṇa texts were written before the time of the Buddha, who took birth in 13th century BCE as per our calculations. Megasthenes, who came to India in the 3rd century BCE, said the following about the Āndhras [21]:

> *"Next come the Andarae, a still more powerful race, which possesses numerous villages, and thirty towns defended by walls and towers, and which supplies its king with an army of 100,000 infantry, 2,000 cavalry, and 1,000 elephants."*

Obviously, the Āndhras were a powerful group of people in the 3rd century BCE. In the inscriptions of Devānāmpriya Priyadarśī or Kumāragupta I, who ruled towards the end of 3rd century BCE and the beginning of 2nd century BCE, Āndhras have been grouped together with Pulinda in the 13th Rock Edict, while Chola, Pāṇḍya, Satiyaputra and Keralaputra are grouped together in the 2nd Rock Edict. Identification of Satiyaputra is not very clear, though clearly they were in South India as evident from their grouping with Chola, Pāṇḍya and Keralaputra. Satiyaputra may refer to Sātavāhanas as opined by some historians [22].

In the light of the information presented above, we can conclude that the Āndhras and the Sātavāhanas were totally different dynasties, which perhaps shared the last name, resulting in confusion about them belonging to the same dynasty. Chronologically, the Āndhras ruled several centuries earlier than the Sātavāhanas. Geographically, the Āndhras had their base in the eastern part of South India, while the Sātavāhanas had their base in the western part of South India. After the fall of the Kaṇvas, there remained no central authority in North India, while the Āndhras became the most prominent power in South India. Seeing that there was no paramount power in North India, the Persian Achaemenid emperor Darius I attacked the western borders of India around 515 BCE and added the areas around Indus valley from Gāndhara to modern day Karachi to his empire.

7.4 Ādi Śankarāchārya

It was in these troubled times that a man of unparalleled intellectual brilliance and spiritual vision rose to unite India culturally. We know him as Ādi Śankarāchārya, and what he achieved in merely 32 years of his life is almost superhuman. Born in 509 BCE (as per tradition) in Kaladi in present day Kerala, he travelled across all of India to spread the doctrine of Advaita Vedānta. He challenged the proponents of Mimānsā, Sāṅkhya and Buddhism for debate and defeated them. This is the true intellectual tradition of India. Hindus did not propagate the notion that all ideologies are true/valid. Respect for one's worldview had to be earned. Ideologies were open to challenge and their proponents had to defend their ideologies in open debate. If they lost the debate, they were supposed to become the disciple of their challenger. Ādi Śaṅkarāchārya established four monasteries in the four corners of India to uphold and defend Hinduism. When he passed away in 477 BCE, he had already ensured that the light of the Vedas would continue to illuminate and guide generations of Hindus.

7.5 The Nāga Kingdoms

After the fall of the Kaṇvas, North India remained without a single paramount ruler till the formation of the Gupta Empire. According to the Purāṇas, a number of Nāga kings were ruling in North India before the rise of the Imperial Guptas [23]:

> *"Hear also the future kings of Vidiśā. Bhogin, son of the Naga king Śeṣa, will be king, conqueror of his enemies' cities, a king who will exalt the Nāga family. Sadāchandra, and Chandrāṃśa who will be a second Nakhavant, then Dhanadharman, and Vaṅgara is remembered as the fourth. Then Bhūtinanda will reign in the Vaidiśa kingdom. ... Nine Nāka kings will enjoy the city Champāvatī; and 7 Nāgas will enjoy the charming city Mathura. Kings born of the Gupta race will enjoy all these territories, namely, along the Ganges, Prayāga, Sāketa, and the Magadhas."*

According to this text Nāga kings were ruling at Vidiśā, Champāvatī and Mathura. As nine Nāga kings ruled at Champāvatī and seven Nāga kings ruled at Mathura before their defeat by Chandragupta I and Samudragupta in the last quarter of the 4th century BCE, these Nāga kingdoms were established some time in the 5th century BCE. What is very interesting is that there was a Nāga king named Chandrāṃśa, who ruled at Vidiśā. He has been called a second Nakhavant in the Purāṇas. Nakha means nails and Nakhavant means a nail-cutter or a barber, as barbers also take care of nails in India [27]. In Chandrāṃśa, we then have the Xandrames of the Greek writers, who was ruling over the confederacy of Nāga kingdoms in North India at the time of Alexander's invasion. According to Greek writers, Xandrames was the son of a barber, who had usurped the kingdom [28-29]. Thus there is a striking match between the name and description of Xandrames by Greek writers with the name and description of Chandrāṃśa in the Purāṇas.

Alexander attacked the Persian Empire in 334 BCE, and as he moved towards India, alarm bells started ringing all over India. Magadha was a tiny principality then shorn of its ancient glory, but its people still remembered the days of the Nanda and Maurya empires. A man from the kingdom of Magadha travelled all the way to the frontiers of India to take stock of the situation first-hand. He even enlisted himself in Alexander's army and urged the Indians in his army to revolt. The name of this heroic man was Chandragupta – the Sandrokottos of the Greeks.

Let us continue with the reconstruction of Indian history in the next volume in this series, "India after Alexander: The Age of Vikramādityas", where we will begin with the invasion of India by Alexander the Great, and the resistance he faced from a fearless king named Porus. The fearless act of Porus was followed by a series of brave response by rulers, who called themselves Vikramāditya. The Vikrama era was constituted in the name of one of those Vikramādityas, and we will identify him. His courage and valor were legendary and he defeated the invaders by chasing them all the way to Bactria. His exploits made him a hero of the masses, who made him immortal in the legends of Vikrama and Vetāla.

We started this work with a quote from Swāmī Vivekānanda and we shall end this volume with another quote from him:

> *"The only religion that ought to be taught is the religion of fearlessness. Either in this world or in the world of religion, it is true that fear is sure cause of degradation and sin. It is fear that brings misery, fear that brings death, fear that breeds evil. And what causes fear? Ignorance of your own nature."*

Notes

1. Tod (1920): lvi-lvii.
2. Sachau (1910): 104.
3. Sachau (1910): 103.
4. Mahābhārata, Ādi Parva, 11.13-16.
5. Bakker (2010): 1-17.
6. Sachau (1910): 19-20.
7. Beal (1906): 69.
8. Sachau (1910): 23.
9. Fleet (1888): 85.
10. McCrindle (1877): 210.
11. McCrindle (1877): 40.
12. Srivastava (2007): 123-130.
13. Jayaswal (1934): 14.
14. Pargiter (1913): 69-71.
15. Majumdar et al. (2001): 54-100.
16. Fergusson (1876): 716.
17. Olivelle (2006): 70-71.
18. Majumdar et al. (2001): 95-100.
19. Jayaswal (1934): 18-19.
20. Jayaswal (1934): 19.
21. McCrindle (1877): 138.
22. Sen (1999): 172.
23. Pargiter (1913): 72-73.
24. Sethna (1989): 183.
25. McCrindle (1893): 221-222.
26. Sethna (1989): 281-282.

BIBLIOGRAPHY

Agnihotry, V. K. (Chief Editor). (2010). Indian History. 26th edition. Mumbai, India: Allied publishers.

Alcock, S. E. (editor). (2001). Empires: Perspectives from Archaeology and History. Cambridge, UK: Cambridge University Press.

Avari, B. (2007). India: The Ancient Past: A history of the Indian sub-continent from c. 7000 BC to CE 1200. Abingdon, Oxon, UK: Routledge.

Bagchi, J. (1993). The history and culture of the Pālas of Bengal and Bihar. New Delhi, India: Abhinav Publications.

Bakker, H. (2010). The Hindu Religion and War. in: Dijk, Jacobus van (editor), Onder Orchideeën, Nieuwe Oogst uit de Tuin der Geesteswetenschappen te Groningen. Groningen, Netherlands: Barkhuis Publishing.

Barua, B.M. (1968). Asoka and his inscriptions, Part I. 3rd edition. Calcutta, India: New Age Publishers Private Limited.

Basham, A.L. (1982). Aśoka and Buddhism – A Reexamination. The Journal of the International Association of Buddhistic Studies, 5 (1): 131-143.

Beal, S. (1906). Si-Yu-Ki: Buddhist Records of the Western World, Volume I. London, UK: Kegan Paul, Trench, Trubner and Co Ltd.

Beal, S. (1911). The Life of Hiuen Tsiang by the Shaman Hwui Li. London, UK: Kegan Paul, Trench, Trubner and Co Ltd.

Bernholz, P. and Valubel, R. (Editors). (2014). Explaining Monetary and Financial Innovation: A Historical Analysis. Switzerland: Springer International.

Cadene, P. and Dumortier, B. (2013). Atlas of the Gulf States. Boston, Massachusetts, USA: Brill.

Charpentier, J. (1931). Antiochus, King of the Yavanas. Bulletin of the School of Oriental Studies, 6 (2): 303-321.

Cunningham, A. (1871). The Ancient Geography of India. London, UK: Trubner and Co.

Cunningham, A. (1879). Corpus Inscriptionum Indicarum, Vol. I: Inscriptions of Aśoka. Calcutta, India: Office of the Superintendent of Government Printing.

Cunningham, A. (1883). Book of Indian Eras, with Tables for calculating Indian Dates. London, UK: Thacker, Spink and Co.

Dāji, B. (1865). Brief notes on the age and authenticity of the work of Āryabhaṭa, Varāhamihira, Brahmagupta, Bhaṭṭotpala, and Bhāskarāchārya. Journal of the Royal Asiatic Society of Great Britain & Ireland, New Series, Volume the First: 392-418.

Davids, T. W. R. (1877). International Numismata Orientalia: On the Ancient Coins and Measures of Ceylon. London, UK: Trubner & Co.

Falk, H. (2001). The yuga of Sphujiddhvaja and the era of the Kuṣāṇas. Silk Road Art and Archaeology, 7, 121-136.

Falk, H. and Bennett, C. (2009). Macedonian Intercalary Months and the Era of Azes. Acta Orientalia, 70, 197-216.

Fergusson, J. (1876). History of Indian and Eastern Architecture. London, UK: John Murray.

Fleet, J. F. (1888). Corpus Inscriptionum Indicarum, Vol. III: Inscriptions of the Early Guptas. Calcutta, India: Government of India, Central Publications Branch.

Francklin, W. (1815). Inquiry concerning the site of ancient Palibothra. London, UK: Black and Co., 1815.

Ganguli, D. K. (1987). The Imperial Guptas and Their Times. New Delhi, India: Abhinav Publications.

Ganguli, D. K. (1994). Ancient India, History and archaeology. New Delhi, India: Abhinav Publications.

Goyala, S. (1986). Harśa Śīlāditya (in Hindi). Meerut, U.P., India: Kusumāñjali Prakāśana.

Goyala, S. (1987a). Gupta Sāmrājya kā Itihāsa (in Hindi). Meerut, U.P., India: Kusumāñjali Prakāśana.

Goyala, S. (1987b). Samudragupta Parākramāṅka (in Hindi). Meerut, U.P., India: Kusumāñjali Prakāśana.

Goyala, S. (1988). Prāchīna Bhārata kā Itihāsa, Vol. 2: Gupta aur Vākāṭaka Sāmrājyon kā Yuga (in Hindi). Meerut, U.P., India: Kusumāñjali Prakāśana.

Hamilton, H.C. (1892). The Geography of Strabo. Volume 1. London, UK: George Bell and Sons.

Hultzsch, E. (1914). The Date of Aśoka. Journal of the Royal Asiatic Society of Great Britain and Ireland, October: 943-951.

Hultzsch, E. (1925). Corpus Inscriptionum Indicarum, Vol. I: Inscriptions of Asoka. New Edition. Oxford, UK: Printed for the Government of India at the Clarendon Press.

Jayaswal, K.P. (1934). An Imperial History of India in a Sanskrit Text. Revised by Rahula Sankrityayana. Lahore, United India: Motilal Banarsi Dass.

Jones, W. (1793). The Tenth Anniversary Discourse. Asiatick Researches or Transactions of the Society Instituted in Bengal, 4, xii-xiv.

Jones, W. (1807). On the Chronology of the Hindus. Asiatick Researches or Transactions of the Society Instituted in Bengal, 2, 111-147.

Kumar, V., Sreenadh, O., and Hegde, S.G. (2013). Lagna Varahi (by Varahamihira). India: Ancient Indian Astrology Foundation.

Legge, J. (1886). A Record of Buddhistic Kingdoms, Being an Account by the Chinese Monk Fa-Hien of His Travels in India and Ceylon (A.D. 399-414) in Search of the Buddhistic Books of Discipline. Oxford, UK: Clarendon Press.

Loeschner, H. (2008). Notes on the Yuezhi – Kushan relationship and Kushan chronology. Oriental Numismatic Society, 1-28.

Majumdar, R. C. (1977). Ancient India. Eighth Edition. Delhi, India: Motilal Banarasidass.

Majumdar, R. C. and Altekar, A. S. (editors). (1967). The Vakataka-Gupta Age. , Delhi, India: Motilal Banarasidass.

Majumdar, R.C., Pusalker, A.D. and Majumdar A.K. (Editors). (1993). The History and Culture of the Indian People, Volume IV: The Age of Imperial Kanauj. 4th Edition. Mumbai, India: Bharatiya Vidya Bhavan.

Majumdar, R.C., Pusalker, A.D. and Majumdar A.K. (Editors). (1996). The History and Culture of the Indian People, Volume I: The Vedic Age. 6th Edition. Mumbai, India: Bharatiya Vidya Bhavan.

Majumdar, R.C., Pusalker, A.D. and Majumdar A.K. (Editors). (1997). The History and Culture of the Indian People, Volume III: The Classical Age. 5th Edition. Mumbai, India: Bharatiya Vidya Bhavan.

Majumdar, R.C., Pusalker, A.D. and Majumdar A.K. (Editors). (2001). The History and Culture of the Indian People, Volume II: The Age of Imperial Unity. 7th Edition. Mumbai, India: Bharatiya Vidya Bhavan.

Marshall, J. (2013). A Guide to Taxila. First Paperback edition. New York, USA: Cambridge University Press.

McCrindle, J. W. (1877). Ancient India as Described by Megasthenes and Arrian. London, UK: Trubner & Co.

McCrindle, J. W. (1885). Ancient India as Described by Ptolemy. Calcutta, India: Thacker, Spink and Co.

McCrindle, J. W. (1893). The Invasion of India by Alexander the Great. Westminster, UK: Archibald Constable and Co.

McCrindle, J. W. (1901). Ancient India as Described in Classical Literature. Westminster, UK: Archibald Constable and Co.

Middleton, J. (2015). World monarchies and dynasties. New York, USA: Routledge.

Mirashi, V.V. (editor). (1955). Corpus Inscriptionum Indicarum, Vol. IV, Part 1: Inscriptions of the Kalachuri-Chedi era. New Delhi, India: Archaeological Survey of India.

Mirashi, V.V. (editor). (1963). Corpus Inscriptionum Indicarum, Vol. V, Inscriptions of the Vākāṭakas. New Delhi, India: Archaeological Survey of India.

Mukhopadhyaya, S. (1963). The Aśokavadana. Delhi, India: Sahitya Akademi.

Murray, H. (1844). An Encyclopaedia of Geography. London, UK: Longman, Brown, Green, and Longmans.

Olivelle, P. (Editor). (2006). Between the Empires: Society in India 300 BCE to 400 CE. New York, USA: Oxford University Press.

Pal, P. (1986). Indian Sculpture, Volume 1: circa 500 B.C.-A.D. 700. Los Angeles, USA: Los Angeles County Museum of Art and University of California Press.

Pargiter, F. E. (1913). The Purana Text of the Dynasties of the Kali Age. London, UK: Humphrey Milford and Oxford University Press.

Prinsep, J. (1837). Interpretation of the most ancient of the inscriptions on the pillar called the lat of Feroz Shah, near Delhi, and of the Allahabad, Radhia and Mattiah pillar, or lat, inscriptions which agree therewith. Journal of Royal Asiatic Society of Bengal, July: 566-609.

Prinsep, J. (1838a). Discovery of the name of Antiochus the Great, in two of the edicts of Aśoka, king of India. Journal of Royal Asiatic Society of Bengal, February: 156-167.

Prinsep, J. (1838b). On the edicts of Piyadasi, or Aśoka, the Buddhist monarch of India, preserved on the Girnar rock in the Gujerat peninsula, and on the Dhauli rock in Cuttack; with the discovery of Ptolemy's name therein. Journal of Royal Asiatic Society of Bengal, March: 219-282.

Rennell, J. (1788). Memoirs of a map of Hindoostan. London, UK: M. Brown.

Robins, R.H. (2013). General Linguistics. 4th edition. New York, USA: Routledge.

Sachau, E. C. (1910). Alberuni's India. Vol. 1. London, UK: Kegan Paul, Trench, Trubner & Co. Ltd.

Sagar, K. C. (1992). Foreign Influence on Ancient India. New Delhi, India: Northern Book Centre.

Sarton, G. (1993). Hellenistic Science and Culture in the Last three Centuries B.C. Toronto, Canada: General Publishing Company.

Sen, S. N. (1999). Ancient Indian History and Civilization. Second Edition. New Delhi, India: New Age International Publishers.

Sethna, K. D. (1989). Ancient India in a New Light. New Delhi, India: Aditya Prakashana.

Sethna, K. D. (2000). Problems of Ancient India. New Delhi, India: Aditya Prakashana.

Shastri, A.M. (Editor). (1999). The Age of the Satavahanas. Vol. I. New Delhi, India: Aryan Books International.

Sircar, D.C. (1969). Ancient Malwā and the Vikramāditya Tradition. Delhi, India: Munshiram Manoharlal.

Smith, V. A. (1915). The Oxford Student's History of India, 5th Edition. London, UK: Clarendon Press.

Smith, W. (Editor). (1873). A dictionary of Greek and Roman Geography. Volume 2. London, UK: John Murray.

Srinivasan, D. M. (2007). On the Cusp of an Era. Leiden, Netherlands: Brill.

Srivastava, K.C. (2007). Prāchina Bhārata kā Itihāsa tathā Sanskṛti (in Hindi). 11th edition. Allahabad, India: United Book Depot.

Strong, J. S. (1989). The legend of King Aśoka: A study and translation of the Aśokavadana. Delhi, India: Motilal Banarsidass.

Subba Reddy, V.V. (2009). Temples of south India. New Delhi, India: Gyan publishing House.

Thapar, R. (2013). The Past before us. Cambridge, Massachusetts, USA: Harvard University Press.

The Life of Swami Vivekananda (1960). Mayavati, Uttarakhand, India: Advaita Ashrama

Tod, J. (1920). Annals and Antiquities of Rajasthan or the Central and Western Rajput States of India", Edited with an introduction and notes by William Crooke. Volume 1 (Original Dedication of the First Volume: June 20, 1829). Oxford, UK: Oxford University Press.

Tripathi, R. S. (1942). History of Ancient India. First Edition. Delhi, India: Motilal Banarasidass.

Tripathi, R. S. (1964). History of Kanauj: To the Muslim Conquest. First Edition. Delhi, India: Motilal Banarasidass.

Trivedi, H.V. (editor). (1991). Corpus Inscriptionum Indicarum, Vol. 7, Part 1: Introduction to Inscriptions of The Paramaras, Chandellas, Kachchhapaghatas, etc. New Delhi, India: Archaeological Survey of India.

Vassilkov, Y. V. (1997-98). On the meaning of the names Aśoka and Piyadasi. Indologica Taurinensia, 23-24: 441-457.

Venkatachelam, K. (1953). The plot in Indian Chronology. Ghandhinagara/Vijayawada, India: Bharata Charitra Bhaskara.

Venkatachelam, K. (1956). Age of Buddha, Milinda & Amtiyoka and Yugapurana. Ghandhinagara/Vijayawada, India: Bharata Charitra Bhaskara.

Vyāsaśiṣya, K. (1988). Puranon men Itihasa (in Hindi). Delhi, India: Itihasa Vidya Prakashana.

Willis, M. (2005). Later Gupta History: Inscriptions, Coins and Historical Ideology. Journal of the Royal Asiatic Society, Third Series, 15(2), 131-150.

Wilson, H. H. (1850). On the Rock Inscription of Kapur Di Giri, Dhauli, and Girnar. The Journal of the Royal Asiatic Society of Great Britain and Ireland, Volume the Twelfth: 153-251.

Witzel, M. (2001). Autochthonous Aryans? The Evidence from Old Indian and Iranian Texts. Electronic Journal of Vedic Studies, 7 (3). Issued May 25, ISSN 1084-7561.

INDEX

ABOUT THE AUTHOR

Dr. Raja Ram Mohan Roy earned his undergraduate degree in Metallurgical Engineering from Indian Institute of Technology, Kanpur and Ph.D. in Materials Science and Engineering from The Ohio State University, USA. He moved to Canada as a Postdoctoral Fellow. Raja has conducted research and development in the areas of Extractive Metallurgy and Materials Processing for twenty years. He has co-authored 40 research papers that have been published in peer-reviewed journals and proceedings of international symposia. He has co-edited the book "Innovative Process Development in Metallurgical Industry."

Raja has always had a fascination for ancient Indian civilization. Through his writings, Raja hopes to contribute towards the continuity and understanding of his civilization and, in the Indic tradition, repay the debt to his ancestors for their contributions and their sacrifices.

www.ingramcontent.com/pod-product-compliance
Lightning Source LLC
Chambersburg PA
CBHW031547040426
42452CB00006B/219
* 9 7 8 0 9 6 8 4 1 2 0 4 6 *